Software Quality Management and ISO 9001

How to Make Them Work for You

Michael G. Jenner

A Wiley–QED Publication

John Wiley & Sons, Inc.

New York • Chichester • Brisbane • Toronto • Singapore

Publisher: K. Schowalter
Editor: R. O'Hanley
Managing Editor: Robert Aronds
Book Design & Composition: Publishers' Design and Production Services, Inc.

Designations used by companies to distinguish their products are often claimed as trademarks. In all instances where John Wiley & Sons, Inc. is aware of a claim, the product names appear in initial capital or all capital letters. Readers, however, should contact the appropriate companies for more complete information regarding trademarks and registration.

This text is printed on acid-free paper.

This publication is designed to provide accurate and authoritative information in regard to the subject matter covered. It is sold with the understanding that the publisher is not engaged in rendering legal, accounting, or other professional service. If legal advice or other expert assistance is required, the services of a competent professional person should be sought.

Library of Congress Cataloging-in-Publication Data

Jenner, Michael G., 1943–
    Software quality management and ISO 9001 / Michael G. Jenner.
        p.   cm.
    "A Wiley/QED publication."
    Includes index.
    ISBN 0-471-11888-5 (paper : acid-free paper)
    1. Computer software—Quality control.   2. Quality control—
Standards.   I. Title.
QA76.76.Q35J46   1995
005.1'068'5—dc20   94-40487
                                                              CIP

Printed in the United States of America
10 9 8 7 6 5 4 3

This book is dedicated to my customers, prospects, and contacts whose inputs, challenges, and need for information prompted me to tackle the task; and to my wife Marion, who has followed me to the ends of the earth during its compilation and publication, and my son Stephan, who has provided the healthy outlook of a youthful IT practitioner to balance the skepticism of my thirty years with the industry.

Contents

PART 1

Introducing ISO 9001

Why ISO 9001?

Why would an information systems group want to comply with the ISO 9001 standard? Because it provides a clear way to structure your operation to empower your people, reduce paperwork and bureaucracy, constantly delight your customers, and survive in business over the long term.

This book addresses the issues of managing a modern organization within the framework of the ISO 9001 requirements. It will be of benefit to organizations that want to conform to the ISO 9000 series of quality management standards because they want to operate with flexibility. It addresses ISO 9001 from a pragmatic business and management viewpoint rather than with the stilted formality often mistakenly equated with quality. Quality is a state of mind and can be delivered better by people who are having fun than by people who live dull, regulated lives surrounded by slogans and exhortations.

Let us look at the definition of *quality* because our common misconception of its meaning leads us to ignore its importance to managing our organization. A familiar phrase might be "fitness for purpose" or, "does it do what it is supposed to do?" The International Organization for Standardization (ISO) definition gives us a deeper insight:

> quality is the totality of features and characteristics of a product or service that bear on its ability to satisfy stated or implied needs.

In other words, quality means satisfying the customer. There is no room in this definition for high quality or low quality. You either satisfy the customer completely or you do not. As we explore the definition of quality further using the philosophies of Total Quality Management (TQM), we find that quality is totally defined by the customer's perceptions. In other words, it does not matter what we think, it matters only what our customers think. This is the challenge we must all face. And what adds to the excitement is that customers' perceptions are constantly changing. They are demanding more and better products and services, and it is up to us to make sure our organization is fast enough and flexible enough to respond to the challenge presented by customers whose sophistication is increasing daily.

Quality management, as specified in ISO 9000, is about managing our organization with the objective of satisfying our customers' needs. It has everything to do with management; from the board of directors through the chief executive officer and the senior management team right down to the person who is in contact with our customers. If we accept that quality is satisfying customers' needs, then quality management systems have as their objective satisfying their customers, that is, staying in business. If we don't satisfy our customers, we won't stay in business. People change suppliers if they are sufficiently dissatisfied with the quality of the products or services they receive, whether this means shopping somewhere else or changing their government through the barrel of a gun—both symptoms of failure to satisfy the customer.

Arnold Fiegenbaum, a Pittsburg-based Quality Consultant, says that in an otherwise well-run plant, the cost of correcting mistakes can easily be 15 percent to 40 percent of the plant's productivity. Phil Crosby, author of *Quality is Free*, claims that you should be able to increase profits by 5 percent to 10 percent. These are examples taken from manufacturing where people have been standardizing and tightly controlling processes for generations. In the far less formalized information systems (software development) industry, figures quoted by Stan Rifkin (based on the Carnegie Mellon University, Software Engineering Institute, Process Maturity Model) show improvements of up to 30 times. Think of what can be achieved by your organization in providing software and services properly—first time, every time!

The benefits of implementing an ISO 9000–based system are both financial and personal. Staff and customers are more satisfied because the software produced and services provided are more closely aligned to customers' needs. And it is all done with far less stress than with the traditional approach where everybody is too busy to do things properly. Having achieved ISO 9001 certification demonstrates competence as a manager, an achievable objective for all. While the fence-sitters and prevaricators are trying to find ways of not doing things properly, a growing number of managers are committing strongly to the cause. Pick your epitaph: "A prevaricator who lost" or "A leader who won."

If we take quality seriously as a management tool and don't relegate it to some sort of "quality department," we will achieve significant savings from satisfied customers. With our improved reputation and credibility, we will be able to offer our development capabilities and services at premium prices. We will find ourselves being taken seriously when the prime, prestige contracts are being bid. In fact, being certificated to international quality management standards is increasingly a prerequisite for bidders on government and industry contracts worldwide. Continuous improvement in the way we work will help us learn from our mistakes and retain our competitive edge. This includes identifying the need to change our business process sooner by being proactive rather than reactive, implementing the changes quickly, and being confident the changes will work properly. As the customers of the management processes, our company employees will benefit by having their needs satisfied and will grow more productive and efficient, thus greatly contributing to the organization and participating in the creation of a quality culture.

Organizations who have wholeheartedly implemented software quality management systems are ecstatic with the results they have achieved. The direct benefits they hoped for are being realized and indirect benefits such as improved staff motivation and reduced management frustration are unanticipated bonuses. Organizations with certification to quality management standards are reporting that they are winning more work with less effort due to enhanced credibility. Customers are finding real benefits in doing business with certificated organizations; therefore, repeat business is common. Certification of your management system to international standards gives your organization increased credibility in the eyes of management, customers, staff, and prospective employees. Your reputation will grow as the appreciation of quality management grows in the community.

Because you can produce better products at lower cost while not having to compete with cut-price operators your profitability increases. Examples quoted to the author include, "winning all the work we want at top rates, we have over thirty percent increase in productivity (EXECOM)"; "error rate halved, productivity increased significantly (ICI)"; and "error rate halved and productivity doubled (Dialog)."

Constructive reviews provide information needed for our people to improve. By trying harder, following defined standards and practices, and having weaknesses identified and promptly corrected, a continuous performance improvement environment is established. This cycle improves all work being performed, and results in the cultural change known as a *quality organization*. All processes are visible, the deliverables are defined and controlled, and their status is always known. Changes are controlled. The quality of products and services is assured through processes that verify them against predefined standards and validate them against specifications that are known in advance to everybody involved.

ISO 9000 is right for you right now: It will consolidate current discipline within your organization and identify areas of weakness. It will give you a focus on core activities while providing you with immediate benefits, including improved process visibility and more effective management. It will provide the mechanisms to control in-house processes, suppliers, and subcontractors. ISO 9000 leads to less conflict, better employee relationships, and reduced costs. The benefits to the community include better goods, better services, reduced costs. and international competitiveness, that is, ongoing development and survival of our industries.

On a cautionary note, beware the chief executive who appoints someone to *look after quality*. This must be seen as a lack of commitment to quality and all that this implies. If the chief executive delegates to someone else control over the systems that look after the customer (the reason for being in business), then what is the chief executive's job? While there will usually be people assisting in the design, development, implementation and operation of the quality system there is *no* substitute for total management commitment. Quality either drives you or it does not. If it doesn't, do your people and your customers a favor and let them know rather than trying to hide behind excuses that there are more important things to your organization than your customer. You are either committed to quality or you are not. There is no halfway. Examples of this lack of commitment are common in organizations that have tried TQM programs and saw them fail after a short time. These failures are often attributed to lack of management commitment. People were told to set up teams and participate and management was not really involved or supportive. Quality management gets *management* involved and committed first. This is the foundation for organizationwide quality consciousness.

2

Introduction to ISO 9000

WHAT IS ISO 9000?

ISO 9000 is the generic name used to describe the International Standards Organization's (ISO) 9000 series of management system standards. They are perceived as being a difficult-to-achieve target for management systems and to confer on those that achieve them some sort of super organization acknowledgment. They are also perceived to be designed for manufacturers and of no great concern to software developers. These perceptions are wrong! Any well-managed organization of two or more employees can, and should, document their management system and enhance it to address all relevant sections of the appropriate standard if they want to grow and prosper. All organizations, especially those in software development, can benefit from complying with the ISO standards. The software development industry also has available to it a number of additional requirements, which are specified in various documents including ISO 9000.3, IEEE 1298, and ISO 9004.2.

The peak standard of the ISO 9000 series is ISO 9001, which is titled "Quality Systems—Model for quality assurance in design/development, production, installation and servicing." This is the standard to which an organization can be certificated for the design, development, installation, and maintenance of products and services such as software development, operation, and support.

ISO 9001 has been adopted by most developed and developing countries. It is identified by the local standards body identifier followed by

7

the number, although the content remains unchanged. ISO 9001 is known as ANSI/ASQC ISO 9001 in the USA, EN ISO 9001 in Europe, BS/EN ISO 9001 in the UK, AS/NZS ISO 9001 in New Zealand and Australia, and SS ISO 9001 in Singapore.

There are two subsets of this standard; ISO 9002 and ISO 9003. For organizations that do not do their own design ISO 9002 may be used. ISO 9002 is titled "Quality Systems—Model for quality assurance in production, installation and servicing." This also has its aliases in different countries.

ISO 9003 is titled "Quality Systems—Model for quality assurance in final inspection and test." This is used by organizations that perform final inspection and testing of products purchased from external suppliers.

ISO 9000.3, titled "Quality management and quality system elements—Guidelines for development, supply and maintenance of software," is a guideline on the use of ISO 9001 in computer software development. While certification cannot be granted to ISO 9000.3, a UK-developed initiative offers a scheme whereby specially trained assessors examine conformance to the principles espoused by ISO 9000.3 and issue a TickIT registration on the certificates of conforming organizations. TickIT is mandatory for software development organizations certificated under NACCB accreditation and the mark is owned by the NACCB (Chapter 31 discusses certification and accreditation). A certificatable standard for software developers has been issued in Australia as AS 3563 and extends ISO 9001 into project planning, requirements specification, and the development of programming and documents. AS 3563 has been adopted by the IEEE as IEEE 1298 and is being increasingly accepted as the primary certification for software developers.

ISO 9004.2, titled "Quality management and quality system elements—Guidelines for services," is a guideline on the application of ISO 9001 and ISO 9002 to services. As for ISO 9000.3, an organization cannot be certificated to ISO 9004.2 and it is not used during the certification process. As stated in ISO 9004.2, the standards can apply to any endeavor, including the following:

- Hospitality services—catering, hotels, tourist services, entertainment, radio, television, leisure.
- Communications—airports and airlines, road, rail, and sea transport, telecommunications, post offices, data.
- Health—medical practitioners, hospitals, ambulances, medical laboratories, dentists, opticians.
- Maintenance—electrical, mechanical, vehicles, heating systems, air-conditioning, building, computer.

- Utilities—cleansing, waste management, water supply, grounds maintenance, electricity, gas and energy supply, fire, police, public services.
- Trading—wholesale, retail, stockist, distributor, marketing, packaging.
- Financial—banking, insurance, pensions, property services, accounting.
- Professional—architecture, surveying, legal, law enforcement, security, education, engineering, quality management.
- Administration—personnel, computing, office services.
- Technical—consultancy, photography, test laboratory.
- Scientific—research, development, studies, decision aids.

ISO 9004.4, "Guidelines for quality improvement," provides a concise reference source for information and techniques relating to quality improvement.

ISO 10011, "Guidelines for auditing quality systems," is a valuable guide for internal auditors.

ISO 10013, "Guidelines for developing quality manuals," discusses the preparation of the quality management system documentation. The documentation requirements and format are covered in detail in Part 3 of this book.

ISO 9126, "Information technology—Software product evaluation—Quality characteristics and guidelines for their use," defines the terminology to be used as the basis for software quality metrics. The development of metrics and process assessment is part of a series of projects including the ISO SPICE (Software Process Improvement and Capability dEtermination) project, which is now in evaluation, and the European ESPIRIT project, which is addressing a methodology for software product evaluation and certification.

Once we develop suitable metrics that can be statistically monitored, then the techniques proposed by Shewhart and used by Deming and others may be applied. These techniques are defined in ISO 8258, "Shewhart control charts."

The IEEE Software Engineering Standards Collection is another valuable source of information.

INTENT OF ISO 9000

If we consider the way we typically do business, we start off by running around constantly searching for the best deal. As we mature we realize the best deal lies in establishing long-term relationships with our suppliers as well as with our customers. Such relationships enable us to work with our customers and suppliers to establish common system interfaces to reduce conflicts and promote acceptance of goods and services. If we can accept our supplier's outwards inspection and our customer can accept our outwards inspection, then both we and our customers can cut out our inwards inspections, thus saving both of us money.

We can start to mesh our systems together by devising some common interfaces and then auditing each other's systems for compliance. This can be time consuming and expensive and so has seen little practical implementation. If we can agree on a common interface specification, preferably one that has wide community acceptance, then we will be more inclined to work at developing processes that address this common interface. The ISO 9000 set of standards provides such a community-acceptable specification. If we go one step further and agree that instead of auditing each other's systems, we will agree on an acceptable independent assessor to do this for us, we will only have to expend effort checking on specific issues. If we have community-acceptable independent assessors, we will feel better about developing processes that address the common interface because we will be gaining communitywide acceptance rather than just satisfying our immediate customer. Such independent, community-acceptable assessors are provided by certification agencies who verify our conformance to the relevant ISO 9000 series standard. These certificates of conformance specify the business activities delivered from specified places. The certification agencies also regularly review our conformance to maintain the credibility of our certificate. This is one of the rationales behind the use of management systems certificated to international standards. It enables organizations from many countries to work together with clearly understood interfaces. The whole subject of certification and related issues is discussed in detail in Chapter 31.

Figure 2.1 shows how a quality management system oversees our day-to-day development, operations, and support to ensure we do the right thing by making use of defined processes, procedures, methods, standards, and guidelines.

RELATIONSHIPS IN A QUALITY MANAGEMENT SYSTEM

Figure 2.2 shows the relationships between the different parties involved in an ISO 9000-based system. We, as the supplier, have a contract with our customer to provide some product or service. This contract may be a verbal request, a written order (customer purchase order), letter of intent, or formal legal document. We may be called upon by our

Figure 2.1   Quality management system guides daily development, operations, and support.

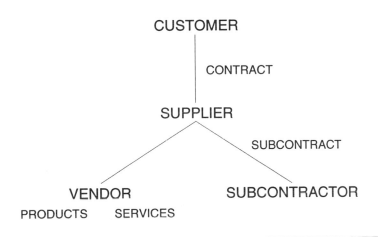

Figure 2.2   Relationships in a quality management system.

customer to purchase goods or services off the shelf through our own purchase orders, or to contract to have products developed for us by a subcontractor. ISO 9001 gives us an excellent mechanism for managing subcontractors and this mechanism is one of the attractions to having both parties to a contract operating ISO 9000–based management systems. Where we have a subcontract we become the subcontractor's customer and the subcontractor becomes our supplier.

QMS DOCUMENTATION STRUCTURE

Figure 2.3 shows the relationships between the various documents that make up an ISO 9000–based system for software development (and other project-based activities). Taking the basis of our quality management system as ISO 9001 (we may include other documents as well), we produce a quality manual that defines our policy with respect to the requirements of ISO 9001. The quality manual then becomes the link (or cross-reference) between the outside world (ISO 9001 and our cus-

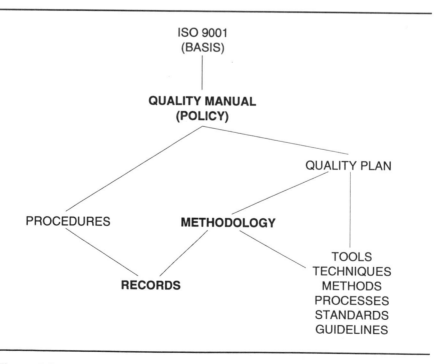

Figure 2.3   Document relationships in a quality management system.

tomers) and our internal quality management system documentation. The quality manual will be seen by our customers and prospective customers. We must assume it will also be seen by our competitors. Our internal quality management system documentation will be seen only by our own people and selected outsiders such as certification bodies and customer representatives under conditions of commercial confidentiality. Our documentation consists of procedures, methods, and standards with the procedures and methods generating evidence that they have been followed and the standards have been met. For software development we also have a quality plan that defines the quality management system elements to be used for each project. This includes identifying which tools, techniques, methodologies, standards, and so forth are applicable to the project.

3

Overview of ISO 9001 in Software

INTRODUCTION

ISO 9001 defines a minimum set of requirements for quality management. It includes Quality Assurance, Quality Control, Process Control, Change Management, Problem Reporting, and Formal Reviews. It ties all of these together to ensure that our customers get what they want by ensuring that the product meets specification and is likely to be delivered on time and within budget. It does this by emphasizing the management aspect of the process rather than the technical aspects. The best, latest, and most feature-laden tools, techniques, and computers can do little to solve our problems without this full, formal management system to back them up. In fact, ISO 9001 with supplementation for computer systems development defines a project management system and, once understood, often evokes the comment: "that's the way we have always done it." In reality, it is the way we should always do it, but rarely do.

ISO 9001 is acknowledged as requiring additional features for software development. This overview and Part 2 of this book are based on the ISO 9001 standard with the IEEE 1298 standard and the ISO 9000.3 guideline being used where the additional requirements for software are needed. The requirements of the UK TickIT initiative have also been addressed in Part 2 of this book.

Quality management system standards identify the policies that should be laid down and the processes required to ensure that the policies are being followed. Each process is required to generate some evidence that it has been performed, thus ensuring that the software development process is being correctly managed. A broad introduction to the requirements of the standards is given below. Part 2 of this book provides comprehensive explanatory, analysis, and implementation information for each section of the standards.

MANAGEMENT SYSTEM

Management that leads the drive toward quality is one of the cornerstones of a quality management system. It operates with corrective and preventive action to drive the process improvement mechanism and is supported by a quality system audit that ensures conformance to the quality system as well as examining its effectiveness. This collection of requirements (Figure 3.1) has been grouped under the heading of *man-*

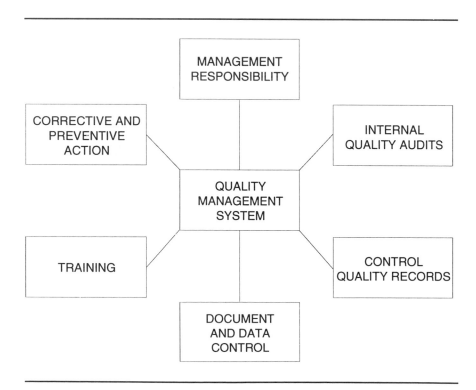

Figure 3.1   Management system components.

agement system and is all that should be needed to implement a quality management system for any type of operation. The requirements specified in ISO 9001 to cover products, services, operations, and projects would eventually be satisfied as our management system highlighted the deficiencies in our operations.

Management Responsibility

There are three parts to management responsibility specified in section 4.1 of ISO 9001. To begin with, management must formally commit to quality in the form of a statement of quality policy. This is usually a letter that spells out the authority and direction for the quality management system. This policy statement should be signed by the most senior executive of the organization interested in demonstrating conformance to the ISO 9001 standard, and should include a statement of commitment and a summary of the products and services covered by the quality management system. It should identify the means of implementing the quality management system, direct all staff to conform to the quality management system, specify the basis of the quality management system (e.g., ISO 9001), and identify the policy documentation linking the requirements of ISO 9001 to the supporting process documentation (the Quality Manual).

Next there must be an organization structure that describes how quality will be supported by the organization. Within this structure the roles and responsibilities of all staff members affected by the quality management system are defined. A management representative must be appointed to make sure that the quality management system is implemented and maintained throughout the organization. The management representative must be a member of the executive management team; that is, the management representative should be the most senior manager of the organization unit seeking compliance with the ISO 9001 standard or a manager reporting directly to this manager. The management representative should have an unequivocal commitment to quality as well as free and ready access to the rest of the executive. Finally management review procedures must be in place to ensure the ongoing suitability and effectiveness of the quality management system.

Quality System

It is necessary that the processes used to develop and deliver our products and services are documented. Section 4.2 of ISO 9001 requires us to describe the format and structure of our quality management system and how it is documented. This includes describing the quality manual, quality procedures, methods, and standards.

There must be quality plans that describe how quality objectives are to be achieved. The quality plan may be project based as in software development, or process based where repetitive processes are used. For software development the quality plan should form part of the overall plan prepared as a component of process control.

Document and Data Control

It is imperative to control all the documents and data that constitute the quality management system itself as well as documents and data that control the development of the product, including the requirements specification and design documentation. All copies of policy and process documentation must be authorized, have a managed distribution list, and be subject to formal change control. User documentation, including user guides and operations documentation, should be controlled using the same processes, although they are products rather than documentation.

This apparently innocuous section 4.5 of ISO 9001 has the greatest number of failures reported worldwide by assessors with about 20 percent of reported nonconformances being failure to properly control documentation.

Internal Quality Audits

Section 4.17 of ISO 9001 requires that the quality management system should have procedures in place to provide for periodic and systematic reviews of all its operations in order to guarantee its continued effectiveness. Where nonconformances to the quality management system are identified, corrective action should be taken. The review of a quality management system should show that all work is performed using the system and that it is adding value to the work being performed rather than hindering it.

Corrective and Preventive Action

A problem, defect, or deficiency may be identified in any software or document product, the development environment, the quality management system itself, the methodology adopted, or in any other area. Corrective action should be undertaken to rectify the cause of the problem.

The processes, procedures, environments, methods, standards, and guidelines used within the organization should be regularly reviewed to identify any potential for improvement and any possible weaknesses that could result in future quality problems. Preventive action should be initiated so that potential problems do not become actual problems. Customer complaints, staff feedback, and other sources of information should also be regularly reviewed to identify improvement opportunities. These issues are required by section 4.14 of ISO 9001.

Quality System Records

Section 4.16 of ISO 9001 requires us to identify, collect, catalogue, file, retain, maintain, and dispose of all records relating to the quality management system including development, maintenance, and support activities. These records need to be properly managed so that they can be easily retrieved to provide evidence that the quality management system is being used and that all its requirements are being satisfied. The records will also be reviewed during internal quality audits and external assessments.

Training

Section 4.18 of ISO 9001 requires us to identify the training needs of all staff performing activities affecting quality and requires that all staff are properly trained in the use of the tools, techniques, and languages used for development as well as in the use of the quality management system. Training records provide evidence that staff allocated to specific tasks are qualified to perform those tasks on the basis of their education, training, or experience.

PRODUCT MANAGEMENT SYSTEM

The product management system (Figure 3.2) is a collection of requirements that deal with the control of products. This includes configuration control of developed products as well as the control of customer-supplied product and the acquisition of purchased product. The management of nonconforming (defective) product is included as is the control of stocks. Software developers may find that a number of these requirements do not apply to their business. The way to overcome these is described in Part 2 of this book.

Product Management

In ISO 9001 section 4.8 this is called Product Identification and Traceability while in IEEE 1298 it is referred to as Configuration Management. All issues, versions, and releases of deliverable documents and

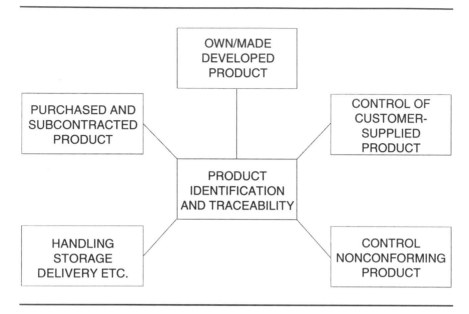

Figure 3.2 Product management system.

programs should be identified and managed so that all interested parties know that they have the correct product and can, where necessary, be advised of any changes and/or deficiencies. To fulfill this requirement of ISO 9001 it is equally important to be concerned with changes to documents as with changes in software components. Note that documents can be controlled using the same procedures as quality management system document and data control.

All products (including programming and documents) should be uniquely identified when made available outside the development team. This identification should include version identification (e.g., date and time stamp). Changes of versions must be managed by a formal change control process.

Control of Customer-Supplied Product

It is necessary to ensure that all information and material supplied by the customer is suitable for use and that the customer accepts responsibility for the correctness of supplied information. Section 4.7 of ISO 9001 specifies that procedures are required to ensure that all information and material supplied by the customer is checked for suitability of use, protected while in our care, and maintained as necessary.

Purchasing

Purchasing must be carefully managed and suppliers must be evaluated and selected to ensure that only goods or services that will meet the needs of our contract with our customer are purchased by us or developed under subcontract. It is mandatory that all subcontracted development conforms to the requirements of our contract with our customer. It is of significant benefit if the subcontractor has a quality management system of sufficiently high calibre to map to our quality management system. This makes the management of the subcontract much easier than would normally be the case and is one of the major benefits of companies working to the ISO 9000 series of management system standards. Purchasing requirements are specified in section 4.6 of ISO 9001.

Handling, Storage, Packaging, Preservation, and Delivery

Section 4.15 of ISO 9001 requires us to ensure that software and documents are carefully handled and stored so that the customer receives the software and documents they are supposed to receive.

Control of Nonconforming Product

If a product (programming or document) is found to be defective after it has been placed under configuration control then controls are required to ensure that the defect is rectified and that affected parties are informed, as required, of the defect. This is the *fix the problem* part of problem management, while corrective action, *fix the cause,* is the other part. Note that the problem may be fixed long before the cause is analyzed and rectified. Control of nonconforming product is specified in section 4.13 of ISO 9001.

DEVELOPMENT MANAGEMENT

The development management collection of requirements (Figure 3.3) includes requirements from IEEE 1298 as well as from ISO 9001 and has been structured to fit the standards to a typical software development project. This includes the life cycle issues as well as inspection and testing and overall project management (process control). There is

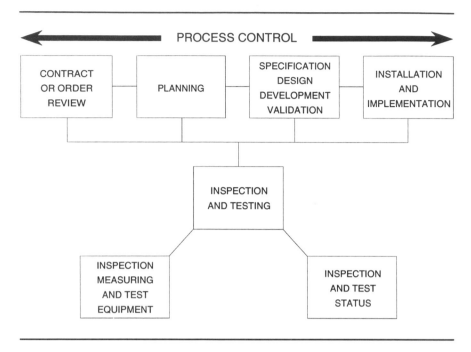

Figure 3.3   Development management.

no requirement to follow a specific life cycle or for work to proceed in series. The diagram is presented as guidance and the deliverables from each phase will be determined by the methodology adopted for each project.

Contract Reviews

Proposals and tenders lead to contracts and also define the constraints under which a project will be executed. Their review must be included in the quality management system.

Contracts and orders should be reviewed to ensure that the skills capabilities, resources, and capacity exist to satisfy customers' needs. Contract review is specified in section 4.3 of ISO 9001.

Process Control (and Project Planning)

A quality plan must be created for every project. This plan should include information on deliverables and review points. To enforce the creation of a quality plan a project should not proceed until the quality plan has been accepted. This plan should be the basis for subsequent monitoring activity, which includes routine monitoring of project status to plan, participation in key reviews within the project, and formal project audits. The planning process should systematically evaluate all anticipated project work.

The process of producing software is covered by the ISO definition of a *special process* (a process where defects in the process deliverables may not become apparent until after the product is in use). As such software development should be managed to ensure that all processes, procedures, methods, and standards are adhered to. This requires us to have all of these documented as part of the quality system and their specific use in a particular project referenced in the quality plan. Remember that requirements specification and design, even though specially mentioned in quality management standards, are also processes to be controlled under this requirement.

This requirement also covers the control of the development environment (including software support, operating systems, compilers, linkers, editors, on-line monitors, and database management systems). All components of the development environment should be subject to configuration control, including the requirement to control all changes to the environment. Programming and document preparation standards should describe approved practices and list any prohibited practices. These standards should cover program design, program coding, program testing, integration testing and document preparation. Program testing standards should include practices and criteria for all testing and inspections of programs. Programming standards should include a requirement for programs to be documented to determine that they are comprehensible, testable, and maintainable.

Process control should also cover training provided as a service, such as end-user training in the new system. Support services offered on an ongoing basis are also processes to be controlled.

Process control is specified by section 4.9 of ISO 9001 while planning is addressed in sections 4.2, 4.4, and 4.9 of ISO 9001 as well as in IEEE 1298 and ISO 9000.3. Environment control is a requirement of IEEE 1298.

Requirements Management

ISO 9001 does not specifically refer to the need to prepare a requirements specification as it assumes that they are defined in the contract. Requirements are touched upon in contract review (ensure the requirements are adequately defined and documented) and in design control (resolve ambiguities and omissions in requirements).

IEEE 1298 requires that there is formal acceptance of a requirements specification. It is essential that the method followed during the specification of requirements includes a means of consultation between ourselves and our customer to resolve ambiguities, errors, and omissions, and a means to guarantee that the requirements specification reflects the requirements and is accepted by the customer, and that the requirements are feasible and testable (include acceptance criteria). Failure to develop an adequate set of function requirements is probably the most costly error that can be made in the life cycle of a system.

Design and Development Control

This requirement specified in section 4.4 of ISO 9001 enforces the formal review of the design, programming, and user documents. It is essential that all input to the design process is suitable; defined methodologies, techniques, and procedures are followed; and the product that will be produced from the design will be safe, reliable, and maintainable. Designs must be verified to ensure the design output meets design input requirements and that the design is validated (software testing) to ensure the system meets the specification. Software testing may also be addressed under inspection and testing.

Inspection and Testing

Design validation addresses the need to prove that a software system works but should also be considered under this section to ensure completeness of the quality management system. This requirement from section 4.10 of ISO 9001 enforces the formal inspection and testing of products. Testing of software should include test plan preparation and review, test data preparation and review, and review of test results. Any other testing requirements should be defined. These include inspection and testing of customer-supplied product; purchased product (including subcontractor-developed product); tools and techniques; and inspection, measuring, and test equipment.

Inspection and Test Status

The status of a software product under development corresponds to the inspection and test status of manufactured product. This section 4.12 of

ISO 9001 addresses the means of identifying the status of product under development.

Control of Inspection, Measuring, and Test Equipment

Where special equipment, tools, or facilities are required, then ISO 9001 section 4.11 requires that policies and procedures are in place to ensure such equipment is suitable for testing the products. In software development, test programs and utilities must be verified as being capable of testing the system. Note that the use of quick-and-dirty programs as part of the testing process is covered by this requirement and, therefore, such programs must be proven to work before they can be used to generate test data, print results, and so on. Other test equipment may include simulators to test power control systems, fly-by-wire systems, and traffic control systems. With instruments this verification of measurement (test) capability is called *calibration*.

Statistical Techniques

Statistical techniques as defined in section 4.20 of ISO 9001 are rarely used to prove that software works. We normally perform a 100-percent test. If statistics are used then the techniques must be statistically correct and the sampling mechanism valid. You will probably need a statistician to implement this.

Note that metrics are not statistical techniques unless they are used for acceptance of product (for example, the software will be accepted if there are less than 2 defects per 100 function points). However, the use of metrics should be considered and documented here even though they are excluded from our quality management system per se. When using metrics, consideration must be given to select suitable baselines (denominators) that relate to your methods of working. Examples include function points, lines of code, COBOL paragraphs, FORTRAN statements, and objects. Metrics can then be quoted to the common base, such as errors per 100 function points or changes per 100 function points. ISO 9126 should be consulted for the definition of terms used for software metrics.

Servicing and Software Maintenance

Policies and procedures are required under section 4.19 of ISO 9001 to ensure that software maintenance is correctly performed. Maintenance includes rectification of defects as well as minor functionality changes.

Software maintenance must be done with the same quality controls as were used in the original development. After all, why bother doing the development right in the first place if we are going to spoil the result with poor maintenance? Servicing includes help desk, customer complaints and support, and services provided by technical specialists, although these are often addressed under process control.

4

Management Issues and ISO 9000

Organizations are now facing a multitude of apparently conflicting dilemmas. They are finding it more effective to break into smaller, more responsive units in order to compete and survive. There is an increasing demand by individuals and groups for recognition, autonomy, and empowerment. There is the need to meet ever more stringent quality requirements as customer expectations increase, apparently exponentially. There are increasing demands that we conform to the ISO 9000 series of standards and other philosophies on quality. There is the need to be flexible and responsive in producing products and services individualized and personalized for each customer. How do we stay lean, mean, and flexible when we are being required to formalize our systems and record what we do?

Formalized management systems such as those required by ISO 9000 can be seen as a justification for the continued regimentation, dehumanization, and proceduralization of people or they can be seen as liberating and empowering people to deliver their best. The result will, as always, be dictated by management attitude, so the benefits are also dictated by management. Unfortunately, ISO cannot legislate away closedmindedness. But even the worst and most oppressive management system specified according to ISO 9000 will result in the existence of a documented system that will enable people to make an informed decision whether to work for them, buy from them, subcontract to them, or invest in them. Formalized management systems can, and should, provide an enriching environment within which people and organizations can flourish. There is no conflict between well-designed formalized systems and a creative, open approach that is fast-moving, flexible, fun, and operates with minimal paperwork.

Traditionally, quality management systems have been implemented in the manufacturing industries where the people doing the work never have any contact with the end customer. We are now seeing systems being implemented in software development and services industries where the people employed are either in direct contact with the external customer or are supporting those in direct contact with the customer. As such there is no opportunity to hide the work force behind a bureaucratic hierarchy and run it by rigid procedures. The success of software development is directly related to the quality of the service provided by the people in direct contact with the customer and by the support provided to these people by management and technical support staff. As a result of the increasing emphasis on information systems we are seeing the traditional method of structuring organizations by function, such as accounts, operations, and marketing, giving way to structures that more readily address the customer. Quality management systems support these changes by requiring us to constantly examine, refine, and improve the way we work instead of sliding into complacency. The challenges presented by the system and the routine external surveillance of the way we run our organizations prevent management complacency from lasting more than a few weeks.

PEOPLE

What is the objective? What are we trying to achieve? What are we trying to do around here? If only our people knew what we wanted them to do and how we wanted them to do it. If only we gave them our vision, our expectations, and a chance to know when they have finished the job we would achieve better results.

Be brave! Let everyone in your organization into the secret of how the organization works. This way everyone knows the rules, the expectations, and the foundation of your organization's culture and can contribute to its development and improvement. If everyone is motivated and contributing, then we are getting a return on our investment in people rather than paying them to attend our premises for forty hours a week.

Empowerment is the productivity thrust that is seeing middle management being decimated by allowing our staff to get on with their work without continuous direction and control. We empower our people by making sure they know what their job is, how it should be done, our expectations of them, and a means by which they know when they have done it. Real gains flow when we make the maximum use of empowered people in our organization.

In the software development industry we are totally dependent on the people we employ. They are our contact with the customer and the customer's total perception of our business comes from this contact. It is vital that we employ the sort of people who are committed to total customer service. Some characteristics of such people are that they love other people, and that they are fun, are inspirational, and get things done. When you have such people on your team you should demand a high degree of integrity and always encourage them to overdeliver. You should demand the maximum from them and be seeking to harness their hopes, dreams, emotions, intuition and imagination to serve your customers. Don't look for unthinking, procedure-following automatons; rather seek involved, committed people. Don't believe that people ever reach the limit of their capabilities; they only ever reach the limit of *your* expectation. If you nurture and develop and train people they will repay it in ever-increasing contribution and delivery. Encourage your people to give you the full power of their intellect, seek to gain the maximum input from original thinkers, and don't be bound by preconceptions. Make use of opportunities to get together with your people to have fun; initiate new ideas and keep communication going. Evidence seems very strong that most original thought and creation comes from two- to three-person organizations where the participants are mutually supportive and nurturing, thus facilitating the difficult birth of an idea instead of preventing it. Use your quality management system to support these concepts.

Unfortunately the *small is good* concept is not appreciated by most customers, so we find that mediocrity sells in bulk while genius goes bankrupt and the ideas and progress are lost. To this end it is important to avoid institutionalizing research. Let research run free but manage the development of the ideas into viable results. Creativity is an emotionally draining exercise so you need to make sure there is lots of emotion in the creative environment. Do this by encouraging fun and laughter as the emotional support system rather than stifling ideas with fear, uncertainty, and doubt (FUD).

As our people are our most important asset it is vital for us to make sure they know how to do their job. This means that we must train them constantly. While people are working we must encourage input from them on how to do the work better and smarter and when we find a better way then we must make sure everybody knows about it. This comes back to more training, including giving recognition to the originator of the better way as well as to the developers of the new or revised product or process. ISO 9001-based systems provide this mechanism through the need to specify the organizational roles and responsibilities, the requirement for training, design reviews, and the application of corrective and preventive action.

Make sure your people can get on and deliver the best service and support to your customer. Don't stop them satisfying the customer by limiting them with bureaucracy, rules and regulations, and complicated procedures. Empower all of your team with the responsibility to serve the customer and the right to demand changes to your system where it fails to serve the customer. Be sure your people understand your vision and their role in achieving it. Place less reliance on following orders and more reliance on self-determination. Encourage staff to operate on the principle that when they see a problem they fix it or take responsibility for seeing that it is fixed. Make sure your team is completely confident of total management support when they try to fix a problem. Then if they fail to fix the problem they will not be afraid to let you know that they have presented you with an opportunity to provide better service and support by analyzing the problem cause and the reason the attempted fix did not work. Make sure your system is improved as a result of the experience. People must be confident about delivering their services and responding to issues that may arise. They must be encouraged to try things rather than talk about them. Again, your ISO 9001–based system provides the structure for this using roles and responsibilities to empower and corrective and preventive action to correct causes.

Make sure people have access to the maximum amount of information so that they can make informed decisions. People who provide services and who support software are dealing with a customer who is not predictable and does not have to follow anybody's procedures and rules. Service providers must respond instantly to any situation and must therefore have the training and the information required to make the right decision, first time, every time.

Make sure you give recognition to your people. Some of them will sometimes be doing better than others, but providing everybody is trying their best all the time then everybody is a winner. Your staff is a team. Don't break it up by making divisions and setting the members against each other. Give continuous feedback and encourage the team to share feedback among themselves. The team delivers the service, therefore the team should get the rewards. Let people know when an improvement has been made. Let them know who found the weakness, who solved it, and how everyone will benefit from it. Let people know about performance above and beyond the call of duty. This will encourage people to excel. Constantly give praise, support and feedback. Be positive at all times and treat every problem for what it really is—an opportunity to remove a defect from your service and to do a better job next time.

Be aware that annual appraisals and performance-measuring systems can have some nasty surprises built into them, especially when selecting top and bottom performers is more a matter of statistical chance than true performance. Examine your performance measures for true statistical validity and take careful note of the work of Deming, McConnel, and Scherkenbach. Do not demean, insult, or treat people with contempt. This is what many procedures do, especially when they insult the intelligence of their user or encourage the nitpicking bureaucrat. Such procedures are a major threat to your survival.

Be flexible in your working arrangements. Keep your organization flat and keep bureaucracy out of it. Build teams to deliver the software and support service. Train them, empower them, infect them with your vision, then let them loose on the customers' needs. Don't try and operate them by remote control. The feedback mechanism is too slow when the team is in contact with the customer.

Teams should be self-managed and, if given the right training, empowerment, and vision, will develop a set of characteristics typical of a soundly functioning social unit. We then find our teams working with significant efficiency. The team recognizes and attends to many of its problems without the need for constant intervention. The team can perform most management activities because it perceives the need to do this in order to survive. This is because well-structured teams are composed of people who care for each other. Look at setting up your teams with no strict internal management structure. Support, encourage, train, and work with your team until you find people naturally adopting responsibility for running meetings, communicating with people and groups outside the team, taking charge when things need to be done, looking after the social needs of the team, providing advice and expertise, and looking after the development and improvement of the team's processes. Give your teams the operational environment they need to achieve their optimum performance and leave them to manage themselves, otherwise you may find that over time the entropy of your organization will run down and a bureaucracy will develop that is slow to try new ideas, institutionalizes research and development, concentrates on planning things to death instead of getting out and doing things, and starts to get the *big project* mentality. If you see these symptoms then you should look at revitalizing the team concept to get the entrepreneurial organizations going again. This includes letting go and allowing the team to take over. All of this can be defined in writing as part of an ISO 9001–compliant quality management system.

PROCESSES

A *process* is the application of methods, procedures, work instructions, and standards to achieve a result. The objective of a process should be to build quality into a product and not to try and inspect quality into it after the event. My personal experience in major computer software development projects shows that walking through compliance with voluminous standards and specifications for programming produces a far more expensive and poorer result than doing things right the first time. Write specifications clearly and simply. Provide a brief list of *do's* and *don't's* and you will get a good result quickly. This is preferable to having a long, expensive quality assurance process after the event. Quality assurance after the event is often perceived as an exercise in guilt assignment rather than as contributing to the development of a quality product.

One approach that has been found to work well is for team members to check each other's work immediately after it is done; this is usually done with no formal recording. To generate a spirit of friendly challenge, a nonaggressive, nonvindictive informal scorecard can be kept of who found errors and who made them (this must *never* be visible outside the team). This encourages team members to try and keep the scores reasonably even. This rapid feedback prevents mistakes being propagated through many pieces of work (for example, nonstandard actions on a screen). Properly managed and with attention to the human issues, this approach can result in a happy, productive, and fun way to build in quality. The next step in the process is to formally quality-assure the work. This has as part of its objective ensuring that the informal checking has been taking place. If it has not, then often the threat of making team members record their checking will bring the situation back under control. The next level of quality assurance is the formal review of phase deliverables. This is the level at which we see ISO 9001 requirements coming into play. This includes verifying that the formal quality assurance and informal checking are working. Problems discovered at this level mean that the preceding two levels of quality building have failed and we should be looking seriously at our processes. Above this review process is the quality audit process required by ISO 9001, and finally, the assessments by an external body. If you work at having your teams accept responsibility for the quality of the work they perform then all quality issues will have been fully covered well before the high-level ISO 9001 quality assurance requirements have to be addressed.

Processes should be simple and flexible as well as subject to constant improvement to make them easy to use, relevant, suitable, and effective. Processes should be defined by the people who are supposed to follow them. While management and experts may initially define the process, they should then be handed into the custodianship of their users who will then optimize them. One of the major benefits of process users/operators owning the process is that bureaucracy and paperwork are minimized. If you don't empower your people to design and change their own processes then you will suffer constant inefficiency and frustration as you battle a paper war. Formalized management system bureaucracy begins and ends at the process level and is made or broken on empowerment and ownership.

The constant change of process to accelerate success does not always result in constant improvement. You can only accelerate success by accelerating the number of changes you make to your processes and change does not come with a 100-percent success rate. The idea is to have more successes than failures and to quickly identify and react to failure. Quality (doing things right the first time) and frequent failure are totally compatible because each time we resolve the cause of failure we get closer to that ideal of *right first time, every time.* Fear of failure is the greatest threat to constant improvement. If you are not making mistakes then you are not making progress.

When you are changing processes be careful not to reject the simple ways; there is often a tendency to get more and more complicated rather than simpler and simpler. Complex and big are often the antithesis of *successful.*

One of the greatest barriers to productivity and improvement is bureaucracy. The heavy tomes of rigid, inflexible, unchangeable procedures destroy any semblance of humanity and improvement in an organization. They require vast expenditure of human resources and armies of supervisors and management. Getting rid of bureaucracy is difficult because the people who supervise and manage have a vested interest in maintaining the status quo. However, bureaucratic systems are a threat to your survival. The nitpicking bureaucrats who inhabit many organizations are a means by which we demean and insult our people and treat them with contempt. Many procedures do this by talking down to their end users, because they are voluminous and detailed rather than being empowering guidelines. The increasing incidence of office violence may well be due to our treatment of people as incompetents while society is giving them increasing freedom and self-determination. If you want to cut out bureaucracy you must make sure all your staff and (especially) your middle management know you have developed an aversion to it and will not support any bureaucratic process. In fact, you should look to rewarding those who come to you with ideas on how to dismantle the existing paper warfare. ISO 9001 has requirements for preventive action that can be used as a basis for this process.

In order for our organization to function within the environment we want it is essential that we specify the roles and responsibilities of our people, and the requirements of our processes as well as our expectations and standards. Once we have done this we can leave people to do what we want them to do. In other words, we have the right environment for delegation. If we go further, we can truly empower people by defining the desired results, providing the guidelines within which we want people to operate, identify the resources available for their use, describe the accountability and control mechanisms, and agree on the benefits to be gained by the organization and the individual. This is supported by the ISO 9001 requirement to specify roles and responsibilities as well as to document standards and processes.

The organization's systems should be developed to ensure that people can meet or exceed all demands placed on them for originality, creativity, speed, responsiveness, and quality. This can be supported by encouraging your people to break useless rules that impede progress and limit improvement. If the management system is wrong then don't follow it. But please—let management know so that they can work with you to get the system right. After all, the objective is to achieve organization goals, not to slavishly follow procedures. This is supported by ISO 9001 requirements for internal quality audits and preventive action.

A problem with most people's understanding of current management systems is the need to implement the formalized systems specified in ISO 9001. These requirements are usually seen as dull, stupid, proceduralized bureaucracy. And many consultants make huge amounts of money implementing this myth. If your consultant has built a monster then ask for your money back. ISO 9001–based systems can have all the creative, go-for-it development and delivery your heart can desire. There is no conflict between open, flexible, and empowering systems and the formalization required by ISO 9001. The most powerful argument for this is the mechanism for continuous improvement supplied by ISO 9001 in supporting failure and institutionalizing improvement. ISO 9001 calls this "corrective and preventive action," and it should be constantly used to reduce bureaucracy, reduce procedures in number and detail, and reduce paperwork.

Properly documented processes should reduce supervision because people can read what they should do, how they should do it, and how they know when they have finished doing it instead of having supervisors telling them all the time, and telling it differently each time. There is always a risk of overcontrol by supervisors and managers unless they either do not exist or have their own standards to achieve, including knowing when they have finished a supervision task. Remember to build flexibility and empowerment into processes.

Do not write rulebooks that try to think for people. This is a fundamental problem with most process writers; they think procedures must be old fashioned and stuffy. Process writers must not think they are paid by weight; they must write short, clear, user-friendly, easy-to-follow procedures. These procedures exist only to empower people, not to train them like performing animals.

One major issue in the fight against bureaucratic system is the claim "you can't do that around here!" Why not? What is the objective of the restriction? What are we trying to achieve? Are we perpetuating tradition or are we trying to run our organization efficiently and effectively? We need to make sure the rulebook helps people improve the process and is not used to defend positions and stop change. One thing to consider is to have an overriding rule that declares abuse of processes for maintaining entrenched positions or resisting change an antisocial act and empowers your people to take immediate action.

Most people think of quality as being the responsibility of the QA department. This is wrong! You should immediately abolish the QA department and distribute the staff into the process where they can participate as part of the team that is not only producing the result but should also be improving the way the results are produced. Consider seriously the role of QA and audit; if all they do is check up and find fault, then they are a burden. If they don't add value to your organization then get rid of them. You should be cutting down inspection and replacing it with increased empowerment of the teams and their members: Quality is their responsibility.

It is necessary to measure how you are performing so that you can see whether or not your constantly evolving products, services, and processes are really improving. These measures should be continuous and as close to real time as possible in order to get the quickest feedback on the effects of any changes. The measures should be cost effective and understandable by everybody concerned.

Look at all possible sources of information and especially at what your customers want to tell you. Look at innovative uses for information and pass it around so you get the benefit of insights from all your staff. If a customer is unhappy then there must be somebody in your organization who can relate to that customer and identify the real cause of the problem. Try not to rely on information that has been massaged for your use. No matter how conscientious your support people, human nature ensures that their biases and prejudices as well as their view of the world will be reflected in the information they provide to you.

Don't always take the obvious paths when measuring performance. Measure customer satisfaction, not just complaints. Conduct surveys and samples but make them real! Set quantitative goals for improvement and new ideas. Consider using ideas, changes, and suggestions as key performance measures.

TOTAL QUALITY MANAGEMENT

TQM programs have a poor record of success, but this is often due to two problems: first, the lack of continuous management commitment as other issues take management attention from the program, and second, attempts to improve processes that are not written down are unlikely to achieve a result. Quality management systems overcome these problems by requiring processes to be documented and by requiring management to provide evidence of continuous involvement through management review.

The cycle of management review, corrective and preventive action, and audit supported by training, quality records, and a documented and controlled quality management system as required by ISO 9001 provides us with a very powerful, self-correcting, constantly improving management system. In this system management leads the organization. During day-to-day operations, problems, complaints, and so forth give rise to corrective action to refine and improve the processes while audit ensures that nothing is missed and further improvement opportunities are identified to improve the effectiveness of the system. Audit also picks up issues that have not been reported or have not been identified because the people using the process are too close to see its limitations.

The ISO 9001-based self-correcting management system also gives us a very powerful tool for democracy in the workplace. We can specify our system with as much or as little consultation as we wish and then use the self-correcting mechanisms to provide democracy. This means that we can get the system into use much sooner than if we waited until everything was perfect and everybody was happy before we implemented it.

The system we document should be generally acceptable anyway, because we should start off documenting the way things are already done on the assumption that until proven otherwise (by corrective action) we are doing the right thing already. Too many people work on the assumption that everything they are currently doing is wrong and that they must have a whole new system for ISO.

CAPABILITY MATURITY MODEL

The Capability Maturity Model (CMM) from Carnegie Mellon University's Software Engineering Institute (SEI) is a model that provides a reasonably repeatable measure of the maturity of the software development processes in an organization. The principles of the CMM have been merged with input from worldwide sources to produce an international standard for CMM. The program of producing this standard is the SPICE project and the model standard is in the process of evaluation. ISO 9001 should be used as the structure within which you define the processes required for CMM. The CMM refers to what is called Key Process Areas, such as planning, process control, requirements specification, purchasing, and configuration management. In order to demonstrate a commitment to perform these Key Process Areas there needs to be a documented statement of policy. ISO 9001 also requires statements of policy for processes and there is a large degree of commonality in the processes required. So we can see that the two work in complete harmony. ISO 9001 is used as the structure while CMM defines the process requirements in more detail for inclusion in our process documentation.

PLANNING

> *More planning shall give greater possibility of victory while less planning, lesser possibility of victory. So how about those without planning?*
>
> Sun Tzu—*Art of War*

Telling people to plan before they start doing something would seem so self-evident that it may be considered a waste of paper writing about it. Nothing could be further from the truth. People seem determined to omit the planning because of pressures and expediency. How they ever expect to achieve anything is beyond my comprehension. And yet, multimillion-dollar projects are still being initiated with only the most rudimentary excuses for plans. Most computer people, for instance, believe a project plan is a one-page Gantt chart and seem bewildered when asked to plan properly.

It is absolutely imperative to plan so that you can think about how you are going to satisfy requirements before you get bogged down in the details of doing the work. By the same token, it is important not to get too obsessed with planning to the extent that you never do anything. Plans are made to be changed and the lack of visibility should not preclude planning. You should plan as far ahead as practicable and qualify the information you provide as you look further into the future. The plan should also contain plans for its own updating.

A plan should always be done even if it covers only the work to be done in the immediate future, including the preparation of a more comprehensive plan. Achievement should be monitored against plans and the plans updated when they start to lose their relevance, even if the update was not planned for. To again state the obvious, a project gets behind one day at a time.

Plans should identify what the objectives are, and how we are going to go about achieving them. Having planned, we must then meet the schedules and deadlines and constantly review and revise the plan to keep as close to our commitments as possible. Planning also identifies opportunities to fast-track our design and development and identify interactions and overlaps that would otherwise result in conflicting objectives and wasted resources. Do not get too tied up on the dependency of activities. Projects with small teams of noninterchangeable resources (such as software development projects) can often do themselves more harm than good by using scheduling tools and computer facilities to overcomplicate something that is best done with a pencil and paper. There are probably only a very small percentage of computer system development projects that are large enough to warrant project management tools and, if history is anything to go by, they have a high probability of being disasters.

ISO 9001 is abundantly clear on the need to plan. IEEE 1298 is specific and somewhat prescriptive on what must be addressed in planning, and ISO 9000.3 has a comprehensive list of subplans and planning issues that should be addressed.

PRODUCT

More and more, customers are demanding that goods and services conform exactly to their needs. We need to be capable of satisfying this need or our competitor will. If we are not fast enough at innovation we will lose out to quicker and more flexible competitors. This means that we need to look at our markets as being more and more refined into niches until we find ourselves dealing one on one with the needs of each customer. In the service-based industries there is almost universal one-on-one dealing with customers even though we often try to sell them standard items. When we have the processes, and the desire, and can sufficiently empower our people, then we will be able to keep ahead of our competitors by delivering a truly unique product or service to every customer. We need to follow the pattern of the world as it fragments into smaller communities with each one determined to keep its autonomy, culture, and individuality. To stay competitive we need to offer more services with customized products. The days of stacking something on a shelf and waiting for the customers to arrive are long gone. We are increasingly seeing that the winners are those who have extensive knowledge of products, services, and markets and provide their customers with results perfectly in tune with these needs. We must remain conscious that these needs are continuously changing and make sure we build feedback mechanisms into our processes in order to stay in touch with these changing needs and respond to them. ISO 9001 process control and servicing requirements should be used to implement processes to achieve this responsiveness.

CUSTOMERS

The customer is the most important visitor on our premises

He is not dependent on us, we are dependent on him

He is not an interruption to our work, he is the purpose of it

He is not an outsider on our business—he is a part of it

We are not doing him a favour by serving him—he is doing us a favour by giving us an opportunity to do so.

Mahatma Gandhi

We all have a customer. Our customer may be a real (external) customer, an internal customer, the next person in the process we are following, or a manager's subordinate. The type of customer (internal or external) should not be used as a grading mechanism to make some customers more, or less, important than others. All customers are important and all must have their needs satisfied.

It is a constant source of wonder to me how much time and money is spent on gaining a new customer compared with the effort expended on keeping the customers we have. We are constantly wooed by advertisements extolling the virtues of products and services only to be bitterly disappointed by their delivery. This would appear to be a totally backward way of doing things. If you look at the top end of the retail market where the high-value sales are made, you start to find the older, more experienced sales staff with juniors supporting them. No high-fashion boutique or London tailor would let an inexperienced salesperson near such a valuable thing as a customer. These sorts of organizations hardly ever advertise because they keep their existing customers and gain new ones by referral from existing ones. This is a far more cost-effective approach than having some ill-mannered salesperson ruin an expensive advertising campaign and destroy your business by driving away customers.

You must make sure that the customer service message is constantly communicated to your people in all actions and documentation. Make certain all your processes encourage vision and innovation in serving your customers rather than offering standard products and services in a take-it-or-leave-it manner. Customer service is about satisfying the customer's needs. It is totally related to quality improvement. Ongoing quality improvement programs should lead to sustainable cost reductions, increased sales, and increased customer satisfaction. They should also reduce the cost of each sale due to repeat business and referral customers.

People who are not satisfied with your products and services tell other people. I tell thousands of people about my experiences with name organizations as case studies. The average person may only tell ten others, but losing one customer and ten prospects is an alarming price to pay for not looking after a customer. What makes it worse is that very few unhappy customers tell you they are unhappy and even fewer can clearly explain what upset them. This is especially so in service industries when bad service is the complaint. We must listen to our customers and encourage them to talk to us rather than their friends about their concerns. Unfortunately, most organizations upset complaining customers so badly that most people are reluctant to complain. They just go elsewhere. Listen to your customers, take action on their complaint, and you will almost certainly win them back.

To paraphrase W. Edwards Deming, we must constantly and forever serve the customer no matter what else seems important. Think about yourself from the customer's viewpoint. Would you like to do business with your organization? Remember, the customer is why our organization exists. Serve them properly the first time, listen to them, be quality conscious and service conscious. Let the customer control the business. If we are concerned for, and responsive to, our customers everything else follows.

If we are still not succeeding, then we are not serving our customers properly. We need to listen more, review and refine our processes, and be more innovative about our offerings. In the customer service model we must rethink our organization. The board of directors exists to support management. Management's role is to support the teams. The teams support the customers.

Customer support includes delivering products and services when and where the customer wants them, not when and where you want to deliver them. If you want to improve your business, a simple way to do it is to get good loyal customers. Look after them so well that they grow; as they grow, you will grow. But you will need to keep your service level up to your customers' increasing expectations. Make sure that your growth does not lead you to lose your focus and start giving mediocre service to lots of new customers. ISO 9001 provides requirements for process control and servicing that should be used as a basis to address these important issues. This is especially so when responding to complaints from both internal and external customers.

IMPROVEMENT

It is important that organizations grow and improve. Stagnation is actually going backwards because almost everyone else will be making some progress. It is vital to keep trying to improve even though you may not always be certain of the results. Doing something will always provide some benefit. This is the heart of continuous improvement. Devise an experiment for doing something better. Try it! Then experiment again when you see the result (good or bad).

When you start changing things, do not go for the *big bang* approach. Rather go for smaller, incremental improvements. Then, when some of them fail, you will not have lost much and will still be motivated by your successes. If you do not have much to show in the way of results within three months, you run the risk of your ideas running out of momentum and other participants losing motivation. Lots of small changes reduces risk, speeds improvement, and minimizes disruption (once the teams are used to the idea of a constantly changing organization).

Move away from an adversarial style of operation to a consensual style. You must be prepared to take the lead and show the way, but involve your people; they will be a great source of input and innovation and you must have them with you all the way.

One of the important factors to consider in managing change is managing the most critical resource, time. You must make the best use of the time available when looking to implement constant small changes. Time wasted dotting *i*'s and crossing *t*'s can almost always be better spent coming up with more improvements.

This even applies to deals, agreements, and negotiations. If you keep the agreements open-ended and flexible, you and the other party can continue improving them. If you are concerned about losing out then don't waste time protecting yourself. Walk away from the deal and find another one that will take less of your valuable time and benefit both parties. Sometimes the act of walking away will have the effect of helping the agreement along. If you are not looking into entering agreements where both sides win then you are probably wasting your time. Don't limit yourself to particular types of business arrangements. Be prepared to listen to all offers and be prepared to be innovative in the deals you propose. The more options and flexibility you have, the more opportunities you will have to grow and improve. Use the ISO 9001 contract review requirements to help spell this out as your policy.

When you embark on the continuous improvement path you must be prepared to give up status quo, complacency, and business as usual. If you don't care passionately about what you are doing then don't do it. Get rid of it and find something else which excites you more. Your job is to get rid of things standing between your organization and where you want it to be. This includes getting rid of bad deals, obsolete or inhibiting practices, procedures, and processes, and quitting functions you have no strong belief in. (The people performing the functions you want to quit may strongly believe in them and could prove to be a friendly customer to buy them off you.) Within the organization, make sure everyone knows the sustainable competitive advantages you operate with. This is the short statement that succinctly describes what makes your organization special and unique and that, when properly nurtured, will make it close to impossible for any competitor to outperform it. This gives everyone the focus needed to generate improvements to support and strengthen the advantage. Document this in your quality management system.

Don't try to do everything yourself. Do what you do well and find other people to do for you the things you don't do well. Subcontract wherever you can; this will keep your overheads and risk low while taking advantage of the skills and talents of others who care for their functions as passionately as you care for yours. When subcontracting, enter into long-term stable relationships with one supplier for each product or service so that they will be motivated to apply their expertise and innovations to constantly improving the products and services they provide to you. A long-term relationship (partnering) will result in quality improvements and price reductions regularly coming your way. You won't have to worry as much about managing a large number of poorly motivated subcontractors and can concentrate on communicating well with the few committed ones you have. Don't worry about contractors letting you down; first, it is unwise for them to upset a steady relationship, and second, you can always quit them if you have to. If you do want to quit them have a long hard look around at the alternatives. You may be disappointed and realize that it is in your interest to work through issues. ISO 9001 purchasing and subcontractor control requirements should be used to support this.

Start managing by walking around. What can be more important to your business than your knowing that it is working the way you want it to? Examine what is tying you to your desk and analyze its value against actually going and seeing what is happening. Be impatient with committees and bureaucracy. Set up teams and task them with accomplishing some improvement. Empower them (and support them) to drive through any obstruction or opposition. Encourage an unwillingness to accept delay or negative thoughts. Find out what your processes contribute to the organization. Find out how your managers have earned their salary. If the answers are unsatisfactory then challenge them to improve. This is really what ISO 9001 internal quality audits are trying to achieve.

Management should be constantly focusing on opportunities for improvement and this can be done only by acknowledging and embracing failure. Whenever anything goes wrong it must be grasped as an opportunity to improve the process that allowed it to go wrong. Make sure your managers accept that things that go wrong are their responsibility. The processes that we give our people to work with are only changeable by management, so when they fail it is management's responsibility. People should be rewarded for bringing weaknesses and failures to the attention of management. Unfortunately, too many opportunities are missed when managers shoot the messenger because they don't want to acknowledge failure. Make sure the overriding policy is specific enough to break deadlocks (for example, the customer is *always* right) and flexible enough to empower people to take bold initiatives. Use ISO 9001 corrective and preventive action to provide the means for achieving this.

QUALITY MANAGEMENT SYSTEMS

The management of quality in systems development has usually been the responsibility of the *QA group*, who are subordinate to almost all other groups involved in our processes. They are certainly in no position to fight the pressures of schedule and cost manipulation favored by most organizations. Quality, therefore, gets swept aside to emerge as significant unplanned expenditure in the future.

The new world of ISO 9000 quality management systems is changing all of this and the community will be the better for it. Only organizations who manage development and maintenance correctly and produce evidence that they have done the job will survive. The ineffective and incompetent will fall by the wayside.

An ISO 9000 quality management system is a formal management system that is part of the culture of an organization. It is not an add-on and cannot be switched on and off at will. You either have the policies in place and manage them or you don't. The design, development, and implementation of a management system to meet the requirements of ISO 9001 is a significant project and cannot happen overnight. It requires management commitment, action, and participation. It cannot be done by the *QA officer*. The system generates evidence that the processes supporting the organization's policies have been followed. It provides proof of project management competence and proof that quality requirements have been satisfied.

If ISO 9001 is followed, independent evidence can be obtained to prove to customers that the management system is in place and is operating effectively. This evidence is provided by certification to ISO 9001 from a nationally accredited certification agency (Lloyds, Bureau Veritas, Det Norske Veritas, SGS, national standards bodies, etc).

Conformance to ISO 9001 should not be confined to external suppliers. If it is good enough for external suppliers of goods and services then it is surely good enough for in-house suppliers as well. The cost savings are significant.

If you don't have a quality management system in place you will start to find yourself missing out on government and commercial contracts and exports. After all, why buy from "Trust Me I Know What I'm Doing, Limited" when you can buy from a company with a proven management system. The reluctance and hesitancy of other than the blue chip companies and public sector organizations to take the ISO 9000 road is rather alarming. Possibly there are many managers who feel inadequate and don't want to implement a system that may demonstrate their capability (or lack of capability). A parallel may be drawn with the reluctance of companies to implement quality in the workplace (safety) until forced to by legislation. They then discovered that there were tangible benefits in doing things right. Be a leader; don't wait to be pushed.

An impression has been built up that achieving certification is a very long, expensive road and that certification is the ultimate goal. My philosophy is almost diametrically opposed to this. In my view the ISO 9001 standard defines a formalized management system that has as its objective satisfying customer needs. Certification is an independent check that the management system is complete and is being followed on a day-to-day basis; think of it as system-acceptance testing. The period between implementation of your quality management system and certification is the time of least change and improvement. You may be too worried about the possibility of putting nonconformances into your system to allow change. Therefore, you should proceed through certification as quickly as possible so that you can get on with using, changing, and growing your system. The benefits of the system come from its use. To this end we use management responsibility—corrective and preventive action and audit as the cornerstones of an ongoing improvement process. If management does not commit to this and instead allocates responsibility for the system down the line, then they are, in essence, abrogating responsibility for the way the organization works, or at least making sure the organization never comes close to achieving the significant benefits available for improving the software development process. In essence it means they have wasted time and money on window dressing rather than investing in substantial future gains.

In summary:

- Management responsibility is primarily concerned with providing the infrastructure within which the organization can grow and prosper.
- Quality system auditing is primarily concerned with finding opportunities to get more benefit from the system by doing things better.
- Corrective and preventive action seeks to use each problem and potential problem as an opportunity for improvement. Unfortunately, managers frequently don't want to know about problems, so the rest of the staff make sure the effectiveness of the system is lost by minimizing corrective and preventive action rather than maximizing it.

We must rely on the above three components, which are the heart of the system, to ensure the processes are the right ones and that they are constantly improving. To emphasize the importance of these: If the management processes are right and operating from the very top of the organization, then the technical processes will rapidly improve; if the technical processes are believed to be right and management pays only lip service to their responsibilities, then there will be little improvement. Fix the management and the rest follows. For the last thirty years in IT we have been trying to do it the other way and are still producing poor results. ISO 9001 will not change our poor record until we take management commitment *very* seriously.

How do you know if you have management commitment?

- If the manager caves in to a project manager and cancels an audit, then you *don't* have management commitment.
- If management is too busy to participate in comprehensive management reviews, then you *don't* have management commitment
- If management does not follow up failure to take corrective action, then you *don't* have management commitment.
- If responsibility for quality management has been passed down the organizational structure, then you *don't* have management commitment.
- If the chairman, the chief executive officer, the chief operating officer, the executive, and the management team are constantly enthusiastic and supportive, then you *do* have management commitment.

PART 2

Conforming to ISO 9001

5

Introduction

This part of the book examines ISO 9001 in detail on a section-by-section basis. Each chapter addresses one of the sections of ISO 9001 and examines what it means, what processes you should look to put in place to meet the requirements of the standard, and the issues to be addressed to confirm that the requirements have been met.

Because of its wide-ranging coverage there is no apparent order to ISO 9001. This part has been sequenced in such a way that there is some degree of logical progression for project-based operations. Reference to appropriate sections of ISO 9001 is made throughout the text.

There are as many ways to address the requirements of ISO 9001 as there are people to address them. The philosophy adopted here is to aim to develop and implement the basics and then to rely on using the system you have implemented (particularly preventive and corrective action) to enhance and enrich your system. This approach has been adopted so I needn't tell you how to run your business, and also because too many people start off with the assumption that they are doing everything wrong now and must start with a clean slate and begin all over again. This is a fundamentally flawed assumption. If you are reading this you are interested in quality and in improvement. We must, therefore, assume that you do things reasonably well now and, until proven wrong, should continue with your existing processes. What proves you wrong? The quality management system, when implemented, will show you areas of weakness and deficiency. So don't start rewriting your standards and methods for ISO; it is not necessary. It is only necessary that you have *something written down in a controlled document*. What is written down will then be improved (if necessary) in response to corrective and preventive action.

6

Management Responsibility

INTRODUCTION

This chapter addresses the requirements of ISO 9001–1994 Section 4.1, which describes the *responsibility of management* with respect to quality. It covers the major issues of management commitment including:

- Quality policy, which authorizes the existence of a quality management system and directs conformance to it.
- Organization, which defines the organization required to implement the quality management system.
- Management review, to ensure the quality management system remains suitable and effective.

Policy

There must be a *statement of quality policy* that documents the authority for the implementation of a quality management system. The quality policy should be in the form of a letter signed by the chief executive officer or the person in charge of the organization implementing the quality management system. It should broadly describe the processes, products, and services covered by the quality management system. These are the capabilities for which the organization will be seeking certification. It should describe the intentions of the enterprise concerning the quality of the products it produces and services it supplies (for example, the supply of only those services whose quality will ensure end-user satisfaction and/or repeat business). It should define the attitude and overall commitment of the organization to quality and the standard(s) on which the system will be based. It should describe how to establish and maintain an effective quality management system as part of the overall management function and direct staff to conform to the system. It should describe the results the enterprise expects to get from the system. This may include competitive position and reputation in the market place. A copy of the letter should be sent to all staff as well as being prominently displayed in the workplace. Figure 6.1 is an example of a statement of quality policy.

Organization

There is a requirement to document a *quality-related organization*. It does not mean a full organization chart but rather a series of generic functions and how they interrelate. For example, we will need to specify the responsibility and authority of the person (function) who signed the quality policy statement, the responsibilities and authorities of the executive management level(s), and the responsibilities and authorities of the operational level(s). We use this section to let people know what we are expecting of them and what they are allowed to do. Within this structure the roles and responsibilities of all of our people involved with the quality management system are defined in terms of their participation in the quality process. Be careful that this section of your documentation does not swamp the rest of the documentation. It should only be a few pages and cover the broad issues addressed in the standard and how these are allocated to the different levels of management. If you want to use this section to refer to the detailed organization structure, then do so, but make sure people can see the major issues addressed succinctly and can clearly distinguish what they are empowered to do.

Empowerment is the art of making people responsible for their own actions and future. Management can empower or restrict staff as they see fit, but whatever they decide they must document for all to see and understand. Reading this section of an organization's documentation gives a picture of how much the staff are empowered, how much authority for quality is delegated down the organization structure, and how quality really happens rather than how management says it happens. This is particularly so when we see who has the freedom to take action on specific quality issues. If we examine these in more detail we see the requirement in ISO 9001 to give somebody the freedom and authority to "initiate action to prevent the occurrence of product nonconformity." In

INFORMATION PROJECT SERVICES P/L
INCORPORATED IN WESTERN AUSTRALIA
TRUSTEE FOR THE JENNER FAMILY TRUST
ACN 009-105-177

TEL +61 (0)9 335-3994
FAX +61 (0)9 430-8224
COMPUSERV 100241,1224

30 MAXWELL STREET
SOUTH FREMANTLE
WEST AUSTRALIA 6162

2 April 1995

Quality Policy

IPS is committed to the provision of quality products and services in:

Software Design and Development,

Software maintenance,

End User Computing,

Computer and Network Operations.

The adoption of the IPS Quality Management System is essential for our continued business success and will ensure we remain a viable and competitive organisation both nationally and internationally.

The IPS Quality Management System is described in the IPS Quality Manual. All affected staff shall be trained in processes relevant to their duties and are responsible for complying with documented IPS policies and the documented processes which implement these policies.

The IPS Quality Management System is compliant with International Organization for Standardization ISO 9001 - 1994.

Michael G. Jenner
Chief Executive Officer

Figure 6.1   Quality policy statement.

other words: Who is allowed to do something to stop us producing defective product or providing service that is not within specification?

Similarly, who is empowered to identify and record any product (or service) quality problems? How about solving quality problems? Who is allowed to come up with ideas for making things better? and then verify that the ideas worked?

Finally, who is empowered to stop the process altogether? Who makes the decision to stop processing, stop the project, close the service down, and so on, until problems are solved and the process can be recommenced? This is a major issue covering the right to stop a production line, close down a restaurant, shut a hotel, or stop doing whatever it is the organization does.

There is a requirement to identify what resources are required to ensure our products and services meet requirements. It does not state that we need some form of quality assurance department or that we need separate inspectors and workers. The philosophy of peer review and team responsibility for quality is totally consistent with this requirement of ISO 9001. There is a requirement for people to be suitably trained in managing, doing work, and performing quality assurance activities. There is also a requirement to provide evidence of training in the form of training records. These are discussed in Chapter 12.

There is a requirement to appoint a management representative who is responsible for ensuring that the quality management system is implemented and is kept up to date as well as reporting on the performance of the quality management system. The management representative must be a member of the executive of the organization unit developing the quality management system. There is no need for the management representative to be a full-time job.

EXAMPLES

The organization chart in Figure 6.2 shows the quality-related management structure. The operation of the quality management system shall be the responsibility of the quality manager who shall be the management representative. Where the quality manager is also a project manager, then quality management issues relating to this project shall be the responsibility of the deputy quality manager (the technical manager).

The project manager and professionals report to the development manager when performing project work. One or more quality inspectors are appointed for each project on the basis of skill and experience in verifying the work to be performed. The quality inspectors report to the quality manager.

The responsibilities, duties, and authorities of each of the positions in relation to quality are described below. These examples detail the

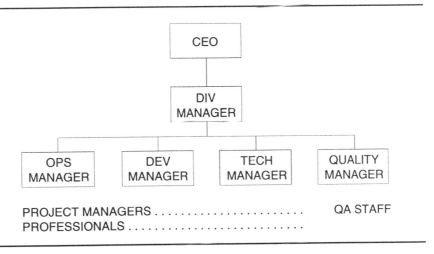

Figure 6.2   Management structure as it relates to quality.

information to be provided with specific reference to the need to give somebody in the organization the responsibility and authority to take the ISO 9001–required actions with respect to quality.

Chief Executive Officer

The chief executive officer has delegated authority for operation of the software quality management system to the divisional manager.

Divisional Manager

- Promulgates company policy on quality-related issues.
- Encourages the development of a center of excellence.
- Authorizes changes to the quality management system.
- Directs conformance to the quality management system.
- Other responsibilities appropriate to your organization.

Management Representative

- Provides a center of excellence in the application of quality management.
- Develops and maintains the quality management system.
- Conducts internal quality system audits.
- Reports on the performance of the quality management system.
- Identifies problems or deficiencies in products or services.
- Resolves problems and implements solutions in the quality management system.
- Other responsibilities appropriate to your organization.

Manager

- Participates in internal quality management system audits within their area of responsibility.
- Ensures compliance with the quality management system.
- Undertakes corrective action for any nonconformance identified during quality management systems reviews.
- Analyzes trends relating to deficiencies and reviews effectiveness of corrective measures.
- Initiates action to prevent product or service nonconformance.
- Other responsibilities appropriate to your organization.

Project Manager

- Participates in the preparation of development strategies.
- Prepares development plans.
- Implements development plans.
- Arranges and schedules required reviews and inspections.
- Reports on progress as compared against the development plan.
- Initiates action to prevent product nonconformance.
- Identifies problems or deficiencies in product or the quality management system.
- Resolves problems and implements solutions relating to the quality management system.
- Analyzes trends relating to deficiencies and reviews effectiveness of corrective measures.
- Authorizes the implementation of changes that do not affect the scope or cost of the project.
- Authorizes rework to rectify nonconforming product.
- Other responsibilities appropriate to your organization.

Quality Inspector

- Reports to the quality manager on quality-related issues.
- Participates in the inspect-and-approval process as requested by the project manager or as defined in the development plan.
- Identifies problems or deficiencies in product or the quality management system.

Professionals

- Ensure all work they do is performed in accordance with the development methodology.
- Participate in quality reviews and inspections as required.
- Attend scheduled training courses.

- Identify problems or deficiencies in products or the quality management system.
- Conform to the development plan.

Customer

- Participate in the definition of product requirements.
- Participate in quality reviews and inspections as defined in the contract.
- Prepare test plans according to the contract.

Management Review

There is a requirement for management to regularly review the suitability and effectiveness of the quality management system. This calls for management to examine the organization's processes and decide if the system is still suitable for the organization's needs and determine if it is still operating effectively. The reviews are typically held every three, six, or twelve months and should examine business directions, changes planned in products and services, organizational plans, and other strategic planning issues. The review should examine the results of internal quality audits and external assessments as well as input from the management representative and other interested parties. The results of the review should be recorded and actions taken to update the system. This is where management leads the organization by use of the system.

As well as formal management review as required by ISO 9001, an excellent practice is to review quality within the organization by making it the first item on *every* meeting agenda. There may, in time, be little need for other items. After all, satisfying customers (meeting customers' needs) is why the organization exists.

A typical policy addressing the management review requirements of ISO 9001 is:

> Management shall regularly (approximately quarterly) conduct a formal review of the suitability and effectiveness of the quality management system.

This policy satisfies the requirement to review the quality management system on a regular basis for suitability and effectiveness. A procedure is required to specify how to implement this policy and the evidence to be produced. The procedure in this case would describe how to call and run a management review meeting and prepare the minutes and have them signed before filing them in a management review file.

ISSUES

When examining your quality management system documentation you should be asking yourself if the following issues have been addressed and whether you can produce evidence in the form of records or documents that they have been followed in practice:

- Is the quality policy distributed to all levels of the organization?
- Is an organization chart available? Is it up to date?
- Are roles and responsibilities recorded for functions/areas doing work affecting quality?
- Are relationships between functions/areas clearly defined and documented?
- Are job descriptions available for major functions in areas affecting quality?
- Is there a formalized system to ensure that trained personnel equipped with suitable resources are identified for managing, performing work, and quality assurance activities?
- Is a management representative appointed having defined authority and responsibility for ensuring the requirements of the quality management system are met?
- Is the management representative a member of the executive?
- Are records of management reviews of the quality system available?
- Is there a means to specify the customer's responsibilities where this is applicable (e.g., computer software development)?
- Does the system provide for joint reviews where these are applicable (e.g., projects)?

7

Quality System

INTRODUCTION

This chapter addresses the requirements of ISO 9001–1994 Section 4.2, which describes the need to have the quality management system documented as well as the need to have plans describing how quality objectives are to be met.

Documentation

Documenting the quality management system means that it must be written down so that people can see a consistent story about the way the organization is run. "Written down" does not have to be taken literally; an on-line computer system is satisfactory, as are photographs. The medium adopted must be one that is permanent, accessible, and understandable to the user. An on-line information retrieval system would be useful to knowledge workers who use a computer to do their work. They could call up policies, procedures, processes, practices, and standards at the touch of a button. For example, even if workers in the food and beverage industry were illiterate and could not understand complex descriptions, they could set up a table for dinner from a photograph of the end result. Similarly, in the footwear and garment industry quality standards could be presented in the form of samples showing acceptable and unacceptable work.

The quality management system defines the policies, procedures, methods, work instruction, and standards of the organization for the management of development including software product, documentation product, and product maintenance. The policies are designed to ensure that customer requirements, including quality, are met. Within this section the quality management system must be described in terms of what constitutes it and the basis on which it is built. A quality management system usually consists of:

- A quality manual containing company policies for meeting the requirements of the basis of the quality management system, for example ISO 9001, IEEE 1298.
- One or more procedures manuals containing the procedures necessary to implement the policies in the quality manual.
- A methodology describing what must be done to complete development tasks and describing the deliverables (both intermediate and final).
- Standards for deliverables, including programming and documentation product.
- Tools, techniques, work instructions, and guidelines on how to perform the work.

Quality documentation should be prepared in accordance with ISO 10013—Guidelines for developing quality manuals.

Basis

Also required in the description of your documentation is the *basis of your quality management system*. This will minimally refer to ISO 9001 but may also refer to ISO 9000.3, ISO 9004.2, ISO 8402, IEEE 1298 and other national or international standards. When you list these as a component of your quality management system you must have the originals as part of your documentation. Don't have photocopies: illegal copies of standards are not the best way to start impressing an assessor with your credibility, especially if you are using the national body who owns the copyright of the local version of ISO 9001 as your certification agency.

Vocabulary

An important part of quality management is *vocabulary*. While ISO 8402 gives the meaning of some basic words such as *quality, quality management, quality assurance*, and *quality control*, national standards may exist that provide a significantly richer vocabulary. It is important to ensure that everyone uses the same words for the same thing, so a quality vocabulary section is highly advisable. When commencing implementation of your quality management system, let the first session cover the vocabulary; this will reduce arguments and misunderstandings later on. If you don't do this people will interpret the documentation of the quality management system through their own understanding of the words rather than according to the official definition. How many lawsuits have been fought over different understandings of *approved* and *accepted*? And how many internal wars have been fought over words we all know or understand? In this book the word *approved* means passed by quality assurance, *accepted* means being passed (accepted) by the customer, and *authorized* means that a record now exists that a product has been released for use or delivery.

Planning

When you work in a project-based mode, a subset of the quality management system is required for each project. This "quality management system for project X" is known as a *quality plan*. Plans for specific activities, such as design or production, are called for in the relevant sections of ISO 9001 but these do not cover the rich requirements of a full project quality plan. Obviously, we cannot produce a complete quality plan at the beginning of a project but we can prepare a plan that goes as far as we can see and ends with a requirement to produce an updated plan. One of the interesting points you will notice in a detailed plan is how closely it examines what should have been in the contract, and what should have been in the original proposal or tender. You will quickly find yourself using the planning process right up front. You will eventually find your customers accepting your proposals as a contract to execute the project. Think of the time and cost savings if you don't have to prepare a proposal, then a contract, and then a plan, and then spend the rest of the project arguing which of the three documents is applicable to what situation. Obviously, plans need to be treated the same as any other quality management system document and managed accordingly.

A quality plan must be created for every project and updated for each phase. The plan preparation is discussed in Chapter 19.

While the need for development methods, standards, and procedures would appear to be self-evident, few enterprises have these issues under control. A programming standards manual including naming conventions for design and some sample tables of contents for reports is not a satisfactory methodology for systems development. The methods, standards, and procedures must clearly address each requirement of software quality management. This means that there must be a defined process to follow and a set of standards to use for:

- Requirements specification.
- Design.
- Programming and user documentation.
- Inspection and testing (software product validation).
- Installation and implementation.

EXAMPLES

The following sections would be found in a typical quality manual:

Quality System Documentation

The quality management system is documented in the following:

- Quality manual.
- Quality plan for each project.
- Quality procedures manual.
- Development methodology.
- Standards, tools, and techniques.

It is managed in accordance with quality management system document control. Records are maintained in accordance with quality records to provide evidence of processes being followed. The quality management system and related records are audited on a regular basis according to internal quality audit to ensure they are understood, have been implemented, and are being maintained.

Basis

The quality management system is based on conformance to the following standards:

- ISO 9001, Quality Systems—Model for quality assurance in design/development, production, installation, and servicing.

Other standards and publications referenced and used are:

- ISO 8402, Quality—Vocabulary.
- ISO 9004.2, Quality Management and Quality System Elements—Guidelines for services.

- ISO 9000.3, Quality Management and Quality System Elements—Guidelines for development, supply, and maintenance of software.
- IEEE 1298, Software Quality Management System—Requirements.

Vocabulary Definitions

Because of the varying usage of words (especially in the information industry), some specific definitions have been adopted. The following is a sample list of definitions:

Accepted   The recorded decision that the product or part of the product has satisfied the requirements and may be delivered to the customer or used in the next part of the process.

Approved   The recorded decision that the product or part of the product has satisfied the quality standards.

Authorized   The recorded decision that the record or product has been cleared for use or action.

Index of Procedures

- Change Request
- Contract Verification
- Deficiency Trend Analysis
- Environment Baseline
- Environment Management
- Final Inspection
- Management Review
- Preparation of Procedures
- Problem Reporting
- Problem Resolution
- Product Acceptance and Release
- Product Distribution Control
- Product Identification
- Product Inspection or Review
- Project Strategy
- Project (Quality) Plan
- Project Initiation
- Project Purchase Specification
- Quality Management System Audit Scheduling
- Quality Management System Audit
- Quality Records Maintenance
- Service Request

- Status Reporting
- Supplier Selection
- Training Needs Identification
- Training Received

Quality Plan

The *quality plan* should typically contain the following sections:

- Introduction
- Management Plan
- Quality Plan
- Purchasing Plan
- Development Plan
- Test Plan
- Installation, Implementation, and Delivery Plan
- Product (Configuration) Management Plan
- Maintenance Plan
- Project Plan (Cost & Schedule)

Details on quality plan contents can be found in Chapter 28.

POLICIES

The policies for developing, implementing, and maintaining the quality management system are covered in the other sections of your quality management system.

ISSUES

When examining your quality management system documentation you should be asking yourself if the following issues have been addressed and whether you can produce evidence in the form of records or documents that they have been followed in practice:

- Are there documented policies?
- Are there documented procedures?
- Are there documented methods?
- Are there documented standards?
- Are there documented processes?
- Are there documented guidelines?
- Are there documented work instructions?

- Is the basis of the quality management system defined?
- Are definitions recorded?
- Is there a list of procedures, processes, methods, guidelines, and work instructions used to implement the policies?
- Are there clear references in the policies to the relevant procedures, processes, methods, guidelines, and work instructions required to implement the policies?
- Is referencing carried throughout the documentation as you are referred from policy to process to standard, etc.?
- For project-based work, is a quality plan generated for each project?
- Does the quality plan clearly reference the relevant procedures, processes, methods, guidelines, and work instructions required to implement the plan?
- Does the quality plan specify the roles and responsibilities of all parties, especially customers' responsibilities?
- Does the quality plan include:
  - Organizational and technical interfaces?
  - Quality issues, including:
    - Methods, procedures, work instructions, and standards?
    - Inspection and testing tools?
    - Development cycle?
    - Review, inspection, and test requirements?
    - Development environment?
  - Development plan, including:
    - Phases?
    - Management?
    - Processes and tools?
    - Progress control?
    - Phase input?
    - Phase output?
    - Verification of phases?
  - Test Plan?
  - Installation and Implementation Plan?
  - Product Management Plan?
  - Postinstallation Maintenance Plan?
  - Project Plan (resources, schedules, and costs)?
- Does the system require plans to be reviewed by qualified personnel?
- Does the system require plans to be authorized before issue?
- Does the system require plans to be updated as the project progresses?

8

Document and Data Control

INTRODUCTION

This section addresses the requirements of ISO 9001–1994 Section 4.5. *Document and data control* is concerned with making sure that the documents that make up the quality management system are properly managed.

Note that the documents and data refer to the policies, quality plans, methods, procedures, work instructions, and standards. Requirements specifications and designs may either be considered also part of the documentation or may be treated as products. Programming and deliverable documents (user guides, reports, consulting studies, etc.) are products and subject to configuration control (referred to as product identification and traceability in ISO 9001) but the actual processes of control are usually the same as for quality management system documentation and data.

Document and data control has the objective of ensuring that people performing work have access to the correct versions of the process documentation. To this end it is essential that all process documentation is available to the people who need it, all process documentation is authorized, and all changes are authorized by the same person (unless this is impractical). Changes should be made effective at an agreed time and the changed documentation should show what changes have been made. Obsolete documents must be removed from use although there may be a need to retain copies of them. Approximately 20 percent of all failures found in quality management systems by external assessors are due to poor document and data control.

POLICIES

Typical policies addressing the document and data control requirements of ISO 9001 include the following:

> The quality management system documentation is managed by the Management Representative who retains the master copies of documents, the distribution list for controlled copies of documents and a master list showing the current version of each document.

This lets us know who controls the quality management system documentation and what information they have available. No specific procedures are required to satisfy this policy although distribution control procedures are specifically identified later.

> Project based documentation and data is managed by the project manager who retains the master copies of documents, the distribution list for controlled copies of documents and the master list showing the current versions of each of the documents. Control of project based documentation is addressed in the specific sections covering that documentation.

This policy identifies the responsibility for the control of project-based documentation including plans, requirements specification, and design documentation. While user documents are logically addressed in this policy, they are more correctly addressed under configuration control as deliverable products.

> If a document has a number on the cover it has been allocated to the person shown on the distribution list for that document and shall NOT be loaned or transferred to any other person. The person to whom it is allocated is required to apply all changes issued. If there is no number on the cover it is an uncontrolled copy of the manual and will not be kept up to date.

This is a statement of policy on holding and updating of documentation. Update policies and procedures are addressed later.

> Process documentation shall be prepared in a standard, consistent manner.

This is a very bald and simple statement and exists so that the process for developing procedures, and so forth, is brought into the quality management system. This policy will point to the procedure used as an example in Chapter 29.

> The quality management system documentation is maintained and changed in a controlled manner with each revision being managed under formal change control processes. The nature of the changes shall be identified in the relevant release notice.

This policy calls for a change procedure to be followed to initiate and manage changes and updates to the quality management system documentation. It also calls for a release notice to be produced for each update that identifies the nature of the changes released. This would point to a change request procedure. It is not necessary to have a variety of change requests; one form and procedure can be devised to cover all the different types of changes required under a quality management system.

> As each change or group of changes to the quality management system documentation has been completed to the stage where it can be inspected it shall be issued for review. The reviewer shall formally review the documentation and shall have free access to pertinent background information upon which to base this review. If the output passes review then the reviewer shall approve it.

This policy calls for all changes to be subject to a formal quality assurance review. A review procedure can be devised that caters for most or all of the reviews needed in a quality management system. These reviews should be modeled on the requirement of design reviews. The policy sentence on access to background information is there to enforce the requirements of ISO 9001. Note that the review should ensure that the documentation is understandable by its end user.

> When the changed quality management system documentation has been completed, reviewed and approved in its entirety then it shall be provided to the Chief Executive Officer for authorization. If the quality management system documentation is not acceptable to the Chief Executive Officer then corrective action shall be initiated.

This policy calls for all changes to be authorized. It may be that the CEO only authorizes the quality manual and each executive authorizes the documentation used in his or her area of responsibility. A procedure will be required to cover this signoff and, of course, a record kept of the signoff.

The use of corrective action if the document is unacceptable is a demonstration of the improvement process. Obviously, if something is unacceptable it must be fixed, but what we are doing here is identifying our attitude to our work. We are saying that if we have produced something and processed it through our quality assurance and yet our customer (in this case our CEO) is not satisfied then we have wasted our efforts in producing it and we should find out why and fix the root cause.

> The quality management system documentation shall be distributed to registered holders to take effect on a specified date. All replaced documentation shall be destroyed. A backup shall be retained on computer readable media.

This policy leads to a procedure for numbering copies of documentation and recording the holder of each numbered copy. The policy also identifies the requirement to destroy old material to prevent people using obsolete copies of documentation. A policy on backing up the word processing files containing the documentation is a good idea but is not mandated by ISO 9001.

> Customers shall be given all reasonable opportunity to examine and review the quality management system. Note that while copies of the quality policy document may be provided to prospects and customers, the process documentation is confidential and is only to be made available for audits and assessments as required by contract.

Obviously customers and prospective customers will want to see how we approach quality. This policy lets our staff know our views on the subject. It also identifies the sensitive nature of our procedures and processes. While initially these would be fairly broad, after a period of continuous improvement they are what we are, and would enable others to do what we do, and do it the same way we do it.

> Customers should be notified of the release of any new documentation being used to perform work for them and any effect the new version will have on the work.

This policy is one of general courtesy for ISO 9001 users but is a requirement under IEEE 1298. No specific procedure is required and a copy of the release notice and a covering memorandum should suffice.

When required by contract or when deemed prudent to do so, a copy of the version of the documentation used to perform work for a specific customer shall be retained as part of the work records.

For IEEE 1298 users this is a requirement but is not required under ISO 9001. It does, however, make good sense to keep a copy of the methods and standards used during a project so that maintenance staff can understand the programming and documentation for the system. There is no need for a specific procedure. All that is required is to remove the copy from the distribution list for updates and *clearly* mark the copy as uncontrolled ("not to be used for development") and as part of the *XYZ* project records.

ISSUES

Examine your quality management system and ask yourself if the following issues have been addressed and whether you can produce evidence in the form of records or documents that they have been followed in practice:

- Is there a system to control the issue and updating of documentation relevant to the standards (quality management system documentation)?
- Does the system ensure approval before issue of the above?
- Does the system ensure effective distribution of documents?
- Does the system ensure obsolete documents are removed from all points of issue or use?
- Does the system ensure changes to documents are approved by the originating function?
- If changes are not approved by the origination function, does the system require that the designated change control function have access to pertinent background information?
- Does the system allow for the recording of changes to documentation?
- Does the system require a master list or similar mechanism to identify the status and version of documents?

9

Internal Quality Audits

INTRODUCTION

This section addresses the requirements of ISO 9001–1994 Section 4.17. The role of *internal quality management system audit* is different from that of an external assessment. Internal quality system auditing is concerned with verifying that the work being performed in an organization is in accordance with *planned* arrangements; that is, in accordance with the organization's quality management system and quality plans. If the quality management system is being complied with, then it will be acceptable to internal audit even if it does not conform to ISO 9001.

Internal audit is also concerned with the effectiveness of the organization's quality management system, to make sure it gives the organization the maximum benefits. Internal audit should add value, not increase costs.

External assessors have the responsibility of determining if an organization's quality management system complies with a selected quality management system standard. While this will obviously include some observations on effectiveness and suitability of the system, it is more concerned with conformance to ISO 9001.

Internal audit can be seen as a form of management by walking around. Internal audit is finding out if the organization is running the way management want it run. In many cases, management would be better off finding out for themselves than sending somebody around to do it for them. If you use an internal auditor, remember that they are management's representative and have a contribution to make to the efficiency and effectiveness of the organization. The auditor should add value and be quick to identify opportunities for improvement as well as to condemn inefficiency, overcontrol, and overly complex processes. All of these are related to the need specified in ISO 9001 for the system to be effective and suitable. If the auditor does not add value then this is unnecessary overhead.

To assist with the conduct of an audit, checklists should be prepared. These checklists will guide the auditor to points that need to be covered during the audit. They may be used prior to the audit or during it, at the auditor's discretion. However, care must be taken to ensure that the checklists do not become confining. The auditor must always be prepared to follow up any line of inquiry that could yield information. Forms and other working records may also be used for reporting audit observations and documenting supporting evidence for conclusions reached by the auditor. Working records should be designed so that they do not restrict additional audit activities or investigations that may become necessary as a result of information gathered during the audit. Working records involving confidential or proprietary information should be suitably safeguarded by the auditor.

An auditor should be formally appointed to conduct the audit to ensure the people being audited are aware of the source of the auditor's right to question and investigate. The auditor must be independent and must not have direct responsibility for the work being audited. The auditor should review previous audits relevant to the one being conducted, review the requirements of the quality management system, and prepare a plan for the audit that addresses each procedure to be audited. The plan for each audit within the program should be designed to be flexible in order to permit changes in emphasis based on information gathered during the audit, and to permit effective use of resources.

The auditor should prepare a written audit report based on the audit plan. The auditor is only responsible for identifying nonconformances. The auditee is responsible for determining and initiating the action needed to correct nonconformances and to correct the root causes of nonconformances. A copy of the audit report should be made available for the next management review meeting.

POLICIES

Typical policies addressing internal quality system audit requirements of ISO 9001 include the following:

> The management representative shall appoint an auditor who shall be independent of the work being audited. The auditor shall have been trained in the relevant audit procedures as well as in the concepts of auditing.

This policy identifies who is responsible for appointing the auditor. It also gives the auditor the authority necessary to perform the audit. Auditor training is always a topic of great interest to assessors, so you will need to lay down training requirements for auditors. These may be as simple as on-the-job training by participating in two or three audits with your consultant or another trained auditor or may involve attendance in a training course. It is your quality management system; you decide what is needed.

> Audit scheduling is the responsibility of the management representative. The audit schedule shall be revised and updated regularly. One full audit of the quality management system shall be performed each year. Audits in addition to those scheduled shall be performed as deemed necessary.

Audit scheduling is used to give a broad view of the audit activities for a year and is designed to ensure all processes and procedures and all parts of the organization are audited. Don't forget to audit the audit process itself (audit the auditors). Project audits may be subject to a separate schedule. Projects should be audited early before they have a chance to head in the wrong direction, and late when shortcuts start to happen to meet deadlines. Make sure you audit important things more often than trivial ones. There is a tendency to keep auditing the easy parts and avoid the difficult areas where real contributions can be made.

> The Auditor shall conduct the audit in accordance with the defined procedure. Nonconformances to the quality management system shall be classified as major (significant nonconformance requiring major corrective action) or minor (minor nonconformance that can be readily corrected). On completion of the audit, the Auditor shall prepare an audit report describing the audit findings, summarizing the nonconformances and listing any proposed corrective actions.

This policy points to the appropriate audit procedure. You should choose a classification scheme (e.g., major and minor) suitable to your business. Nonconformances should be documented and the manager of the group being audited should commit to rectifying the nonconformances in an acceptable time. A basic rule is that the auditor finds the non-conformances and the manger fixes them. This does not mean that the auditor cannot support the manager in identifying possible causes and fixes. You need to be careful to maintain auditor independence but keep in mind that auditing should mean adding value, not picking on every little detail.

> When a nonconformance has been recorded and agreed to by the relevant manager then corrective action shall be initiated by the manager. Dates for implementation of corrective action shall be agreed between the manager and the auditor and these shall be recorded.

This should point to the standard problem reporting procedure. The manager should commit to a date for clearing the nonconformance and this must be monitored. The management representative should have a record of the status of all nonconformances to the quality management system and the executive should take action on nonconformances that have not been cleared by the agreed date. Failure by the executive to take action on late clearance of nonconformances is a symptom of lack of management commitment.

ISSUES

Examine your quality management system and ask yourself if the following issues have been addressed and whether you can produce evidence in the form of records or documents that they have been followed in practice:

- Does the system for internal quality audits operate against a planned schedule?
- Does the system require the scope of each audit to be clearly defined?
- Does the internal system extend to on-site/remote site activities?
- Does the system require the audit results to be documented?
- Does the system require necessary corrective actions to be initiated, reviewed, and closed out positively within a reasonable time scale?
- Does the system require audits to be performed by qualified personnel having sufficient independence and authority?

10

Corrective and Preventive Action

INTRODUCTION

This section addresses the requirements of ISO 9001–1994 Section 4.14, and deals with identifying and rectifying the causes of problems (corrective action) or preventing potential problems (preventive action). The techniques used to identify and correct the cause of problems will be those used by TQM practitioners and include those defined in ISO 9004.4. Rectifying the problem (fixing the defect) is addressed in Chapter 17.

Corrective Action

Corrective action is the process of determining the *cause* of problems, defects, and deficiencies, and rectifying that cause. This means that there must be a mechanism to record *everything* that goes wrong. A common concern with this need to record is the fear of being inundated with problem reports. A much more common problem is the failure of people to record problems for fear of repercussions or delaying the work. A significant part of the implementation program must be to drive out this fear and encourage input.

Preventive Action

Preventive action analyzes the way things are done to identify and eliminate potential causes of problems. This includes an ongoing process of review of the way work is done as well as examining customer complaints and feedback to identify ways of working better. This is often called process improvement and is a significant part of TQM programs.

It is important, however, not to be sidetracked from quality management into a full TQM program at this stage. The formalization of the management system (quality management) is a precursor to TQM. The development and implementation of a quality management system usually brings significant benefits in its own right. Once the initial benefits are being obtained and staff develop an acceptance of quality as a way of life then a more formalized improvement process or TQM program can be initiated and documented as an update to the quality management system.

POLICIES

Typical policies addressing the corrective action requirements of ISO 9001 include the following:

> When any nonconformance, defect or deficiency is identified in a service or released product then it shall be recorded and documented in sufficient detail to enable it to be resolved. Where the problem relates to a defective product then control of nonconforming product shall be initiated to rectify the defect.

This policy identifies the need to record quality problems and should point to the problem reporting procedure. The policy also identifies what a problem is. In software development we need to decide at what point we should start recording and analyzing problems, otherwise we may find ourselves raising a problem report for each compilation error. A good starting point is to apply problem reporting when something is released outside the development team. As the quality improves you may decide to initiate problem reporting earlier in the development process. Finally, it is useful to point people to the other part of problem management, which is rectifying the defect (fixing the problem), by using "control of nonconforming product procedures."

> The cause of the problem shall be identified and any corrective actions required shall be initiated. These corrective actions shall be verified and the situation monitored to ensure the corrective action has been effective.

This policy identifies the need to find the cause of the problem. This is not some trivial exercise in allocating blame or identifying superficial causes. It should be aimed at identifying root causes and taking action to remove them. Root causes are usually resolved only by management as they are often part of the way we work (part of the management system). A whole industry has been built up that offers approaches to identifying and removing the root causes of problems. You may wish to implement such a TQM program or adopt some of the problem analysis techniques proposed; ISO 9004.4 contains some excellent techniques. This policy should reference the approach to be adopted.

> On a regular basis (approximately monthly) review service requests; project, product and design reviews; inspection and test results; problem reports and change requests to identify any trends that may require corrective action. Concessions, maintenance and service requests, training evaluations and customer complaints shall be included in these analyses.

Despite having a formal problem reporting procedure there are significant benefits in examining everything we do and seeing if there are any improvement opportunities or patterns developing that point to potential problems. As with problem reporting we should be looking closely at root causes and not just local, simple fixes.

> Any changes to the quality management system documentation shall be managed under formal change control processes. Changes requested during corrective action shall be applied to the quality management system in accordance with quality management system documentation control. The normal review and acceptance process will ensure that all outstanding changes have been processed in the new release of the quality management system.

As mentioned earlier, most problems are due to the management system and, therefore, correction of the root causes would require changes to the quality management system. These changes must be properly managed and this is done by referencing the change request procedure with its associated reviews and signoff. Chapter 8 covers this in detail.

> Any skills deficiencies and/or training required as part of corrective action shall be included in the training plan.

Problems are often caused by people not following processes or not knowing that there are processes to be followed. The action to be taken is to train the people in the existence and use of the processes. This training may be provided on-the-job, or the need for longer-term or more intensive training recorded in the training plan.

> Where work is being undertaken as a project then the project manager shall prepare regular reports on the status of, and progress made on, each project. These reports shall include the achievement of targets, compliance with the quality plan and the status of internal management milestones.

Status reporting only provides information unless there are problems or potential problems. For this reason it is logical to put a policy calling for status reporting in this section. Status reporting may also be used to provide evidence of process control.

> A monthly status report shall be provided to the executive which includes a summary of each corrective action raised within the organization, actions taken and an analysis of the effectiveness of the corrective action.

This status report records the corrective actions being taken to clear nonconformances identified by audit as well as the actions being taken to remove the root causes of all problems identified. This report should be presented to the executive as evidence of control of corrective actions. Management of this report is one of the most important tasks undertaken by the executive. If they are not managing what is going wrong and driving the organization to improve, then what are they doing?

ISSUES

Examine your quality management system and ask yourself if the following issues have been addressed and whether you can produce evidence in the form of records or documents that they have been followed in practice:

- Are there procedures established to investigate the cause of nonconforming products/services?
- Do the procedures include analysis of processes, work operations, concessions, quality records, complaints, and service reports to detect and eliminate potential causes of nonconforming products/services?

- Docs the system require records of customer complaints be maintained?
- Does the system require preventative actions be taken to deal with deteriorating trends or problems?
- Does the system require management reviews of corrective actions to ensure they are effective?
- Does the system provide for revisions in processes resulting from corrective action?

11

Control of Quality Records

INTRODUCTION

This section addresses the requirements of ISO 9001–1994 Section 4.16. *Quality records* are the evidence that the quality management system is operating in accordance with defined processes and plans "in accordance with planned arrangements" as well as in accordance with ISO 9001; these records are used by external assessors, customers, internal auditors, and management

Each process should generate evidence that it has been performed properly. However there is no need to go overboard with records. Trees look much nicer growing than they do as pieces of paper in a filing cabinet. The extent of recordkeeping should be consistent with the need to demonstrate that you have done the right thing or followed due process. A rule of thumb to apply if you are concerned about records is to ask yourself if you would look foolish if you were required to prove your competence and you had forgotten to keep the records.

Quality records is where the bureaucrat comes to the fore. Bureaucrats generate mountains of useless paper and justify it, and its management, as being required. Unless you are a totally paperless organization there should not be a quantum increase in records. Hopefully, by thinking about your processes you will experience a quantum decrease in records. (If you subcontract work, then copies of quality records produced by your subcontractor should be kept as part of your quality records for your contract with your customer.)

Records may be kept on computer providing you can attest to the authority under which a product was released as passing inspection. This can be done by signing, when required, that the attached computer printout is a true record of inspection. Be careful; the records and evidence we talk about in quality management are not necessarily legally acceptable records. Consult your legal advisers regarding legality of records. The acceptability of records referred to here is acceptability to a quality system assessor.

Quality records management is a straightforward exercise. There is a need to make sure that records are identifiable to the thing that they record; the project, product, batch, version, and type of record should be easily ascertained. People need to know how to collect records and where to send them. If a computer is used to collect records then its use needs to be described. There must be a catalogue (index) of records so that authorized people can find quality records even if the person we normally ask is unavailable. Records must be filed on some media that has to be stored somewhere. For example, records may be filed in manila folders and stored in a filing cabinet. Records may need to be updated by new information being appended. They need to be retrieved for examination and processing. They need to be culled when superseded, archived when no longer required for current processing, and have other maintenance tasks performed on them. Finally, records need to be disposed of when no longer useful. This is always of concern because of the varying legal and contractual conditions for retaining records. Consult your legal adviser on the issue of records disposal.

Quality Management System Records

Records must be kept for all activities connected with the quality management system. These records include the configuration management records for the quality management system documentation itself, problem reports and change requests relating to the quality management system, and other records relating to the development and review of the quality management system, including the following:

- Quality system audits.
- Software development environments.
- Management reviews.
- Training.

Project Records

Records must be kept for each project. These provide the evidence that the project was executed in conformance with the quality management system, including the quality plan for the project. These records must be retained:

- For legal reasons; based on both the contract for the project and the need for the enterprise to protect itself from future actions.
- For the team; to provide evidence for future inquiries, audits, and routine system reviews that correct procedures were followed. This material also assists future reviews of functionality.

Project quality records are retained by the project manager until completion of the project when they are handed to the quality manager. They include the following:

- Project quality records file.
- Project deliverable documents.
- Standards and procedures used (optional).

Retention periods of five to ten years are not uncommon.

POLICIES

Typical policies addressing records management requirements of ISO 0001 include the following:

> The management representative maintains a catalogue of all files containing quality records.

ISO 9001 requires records to be indexed. This is best done by having an index or catalogue of files, particularly those relating to quality management. The catalogue should identify what the file is, what it contains, how the records are filed, and who has custody of it.

> For work performed as a project the project manager retains the records until the project is completed. At this time the records are handed into the care of the management representative.

Project records should logically be managed by the project manager. After completion of the project the new custodian should be identified. This may be the management representative, the company archives, or the maintenance/support manager.

> For work performed as a continuous process or processes the records shall be retained by the process supervisor.

This policy would be useful for help/support desk records and computer operations records.

> Records no longer required for reference or internal quality audits shall be archived with the organization's archives

Specify the policy with respect to archiving records. You will need to refer to an archive procedure that will show how records are indexed and stored as well as how to retrieve records from the archives.

> As each process, review, inspection or test which generates a record is completed then the original or copy of the record produced shall be filed in the relevant file.

This is one of a number of policies you will specify that appear so self-evident that you wonder why you need to write them. There are two reasons: First, they need to be written down somewhere. Second, while you may believe everybody knows your policies it is very often not the case. Many people have no idea how even the most basic things are done in an organization.

> Records shall be legible and kept in accordance with normally accepted office practices and shall be protected from loss or damage. Records shall be available within one day of being requested.

This is an apparently self-evident statement. You must be able to read the records; in a multilanguage culture you may need to specify what languages are acceptable. Records should be put away where they won't be damaged by coffee or engine oil or thrown out by the cleaners as rubbish.

> Records shall contain identification of the project (if a project record), the work being done and the product to which it refers (including versions and release, as applicable).

Records should show what they apply to. This may include a version number of some sort or the date and time stamp on a computer file. After all, you do not review a document, you review a version of a document.

> Where copies of the quality management system documentation are to be kept as records then they shall be removed from their distribution list, marked as not to be used or updated and filed with the relevant records.

It is often useful, or even necessary, to keep an old copy of documentation (such as a standards manual), and yet we have to make sure old versions of documentation are not used during development. We can do this by converting the document to a record by making it unchangeable.

> Pertinent subcontractor records shall form part of the records. These will be defined in the subcontract.

One of the important points about using subcontractors is that it in no way relieves us of the need to meet requirements. This means that any records we are required to produce or retain for our customer will have to be produced by our subcontractor. Consequently, we must make sure we get copies of relevant subcontractor records and keep these as part of our records.

> Records shall be kept for a minimum period of five years from the date of final inspection unless a longer period is required by contract or legislation. A written request to dispose of project quality records shall be signed by the management representative and other appropriate authorities.

We need to define policies with respect to the retention of records. This is a difficult task in most societies where we may be subject to many legislative requirements for recordkeeping. Check with your legal advisers before you commit to a disposition policy.

> Customers shall be given access to all records related to work done for them. The customer shall undertake to protect the confidentiality of all information provided. If a confidentiality agreement is not in force then one shall be executed.

We should be happy to let our customers see records relating to work we have done for them. In some cases the records may relate to some proprietary processes, so we may need to ask the customer to sign a confidentiality agreement.

> Third parties, other than our certification agency, shall not be given access to, or information about, records relating to customers without the written permission of the customer for whom the work was performed.

We should look after the confidentiality of our customers and this can be accomplished by refusing to divulge either records or even the existence of records. Obviously, the laws of your country will contain situations, such as court orders where you will have to breach this requirement but it is not really necessary to specify these in your policy. The identification of your certification body as a third party able to look at customer records is there so that assessments can be made without having a nonconformance raised for breach of this policy.

ISSUES

Examine your quality management system and ask yourself if the following issues have been addressed and whether you can produce evidence in the form of records or documents that they have been followed in practice:

- Is a system established for the identification, collection, indexing, filing, storage, maintenance, and disposition of quality records?
- Does the system require records to be readily retrievable?
- Does the system require inspection results to show if specified requirements have been achieved or the nature of nonconformance?
- Does the system extend to subcontractor records?
- Does the system require retention times for records to be established and recorded?
- Does the system require records to be stored in an environment that will minimize deterioration or damage and prevent loss?
- Does the system allow for customer evaluation of the records?

12

Training

INTRODUCTION

This section addresses the requirements of ISO 9001–1994 Section 4.18. *Training* is a significant part of our drive for quality. We should be training people all the time as we diversify their abilities, enrich their jobs, build a more flexible work force, and improve our processes.

It is important to identify the training needs of our people and make sure that all staff have the education, training, and experience necessary to do their jobs. Any training required to satisfy customer, regulatory, or contract requirements should be identified during the contract review process and included in the quality plan.

There is a need to have records that people have been trained in specific processes as well as records of their previous skills, training, education, and experience. These records should then be used to allocate our people to the work that has to be performed. Most of us are poor at keeping training records and it can be surprising to discover that we really do a lot of training, from on-the-job right through to formal external training. We usually only record the external training or special internal training that costs us direct money paid out to some trainer or training organization. We must now collect and verify (as best we can) the skills and experience of our people and then supplement this with records of which processes they have been trained in. Each time somebody receives some training, including counseling on how to follow processes properly, an informal walkthrough of a process, or an on-the-job coaching session, this should be recorded.

If you deliver training as a product or service, your quality management system will need to address the design of training courses and materials, the processes of delivering training, and the evaluation of training delivery. In other words, training is one of your products or services. This section of ISO 9001 would then apply to ensuring your staff are trained in the preparation and delivery of training.

POLICIES

Typical policies addressing the training requirements of ISO 9001 include the following:

> Training needs shall be identified and recorded as part of management review, performance appraisal, quality planning, corrective action, and input from employees, supervisors, and management. All new employees have a need for initial training in the quality management system. Auditors shall be specifically trained in audit procedures and in the concepts of quality system auditing.

Identify what processes and/or situations will identify the need for training. This includes the introduction of new processes, procedures, and technology. Make sure all staff are trained in the quality management system. Note that training includes what is often referred to as counseling, guidance, admonishing, and possibly disciplinary action. It is useful to specifically mention the training needs of internal quality auditors.

> When a member of our staff has received any training this shall be recorded and management shall make an assessment of the effectiveness of the training and its contribution toward proficiency. Training includes in-house and on-the-job training as well as external training and education.

All training provided should be recorded. This is especially important for training in internal audit and initial training in the quality management system. You should be able to provide evidence that your people are qualified to perform the work assigned to them. Make sure you have a record of the skills your people brought with them when they started working with you. A copy of their resume annotated as accepted by the selection team is a good record of these skills. IEEE 1298 also calls for an assessment of training effectiveness that may be as simple as management signing off the training.

> Our people shall be assigned to tasks on the basis of their skills, education, training and experience in performing the work required. This shall be done with reference to the training records.

This again refers to the need for our people to be properly trained. We often assign people to tasks without analyzing their capability to do the job, or worse, fail to assign somebody because we forgot that they had the skills we needed. This requirement to allocate suitably qualified staff is additionally emphasized under ISO 9001 Section 4.4, Design Control.

ISSUES

Examine your quality management system and ask yourself if the following issues have been addressed and whether you can produce evidence in the form of records or documents that they have been followed in practice:

- Is there a system for the identification of training needs of all personnel?
- Does the system require education/training to be provided where required?
- Does the system require training records to be maintained?
- Does the system require records containing details of education, training, and skills to be maintained for all personnel performing activities affecting quality?

13

Product Identification
and Traceability

INTRODUCTION

This section addresses the requirements of ISO 9001–1994 Section 4.8. *Product identification and traceability* is also known as *configuration management*. It addresses the requirement to be able to trace a product (or component) back through the various specification documents to its original specification. In other words, how can we prove that a product was made to version 2.0 of the specification or version 3.4 of the specification?

This section is designed to ensure that all products, and where required, parts of products can be identified and that control is exercised over this identification; that approval is formally obtained before a modification is made to a product; and that modifications are properly integrated through formal change control procedures.

The point in the process at which products are subject to formal configuration control should be carefully chosen to optimize the benefits of flexibility of development against control over inspected products. As a general rule, configuration management should be initiated once we start spending money on inspection and test. This prevents people from continuing to work on products that have already been through an inspection and approval process thus negating the inspection and incurring additional reinspection costs.

In certain cases the product is documentation. Sometimes it is not even clear whether that documentation is quality system documentation as managed in accordance with Document and Data Control (ISO 9001 Section 4.5) or a real product. For instance, we may consider plans, requirements specifications, and design output to be documentation products or quality management system documentation. It really does not matter as there should be adequate control over these and the mechanisms for control should be the same. That is, they will include proper authorization, version control, change control, and distribution control. For the purposes of drawing a line between quality management system documentation and documentation product, you might look on quality management system documentation as anything contributing to the quality of what we deliver to the customer and documentation product as any document we deliver to the customer to satisfy their requirement. To this end quality management system documentation would include plans, requirements specifications, and design output, as these are all part of the definition of what we have to produce in terms of user guides, operations manuals, and computer programming. We also deliver the requirements specification and design documentation, but this is to enable customers to take over the ongoing maintenance of the product we have developed.

POLICIES

Typical policies addressing product identification and traceability requirements of ISO 9001 include the following:

> When a product or manageable part of a product is to be produced then all relevant identification information shall be recorded including the source of specification and design. The identification of versions shall be as defined in the contract or in the product identification procedure. The identification of documentation product is normally by version number with revisions being identified by revision letter.

We need to identify our products with an ability to trace back to the original specification. In software development we usually have very clear traceability from the requirements specification to the design/programming specification through to the programming. This may prove more difficult with some techniques than with others. This is particularly so where we may have difficulty relating objects back to user requirements. The IEEE software engineering standards have some good information on the procedures necessary, but do not fall into the trap of meeting excessive DoD type configuration control if it adds no value to the work you are doing for your customer. A product register identifying file number, version number (e.g., date and time stamp), and source of requirement is a reasonable starting point.

> When a product has been approved and accepted then it shall be identified as released by an authorized record showing the current version.

This can be as simple as adding a status field to the product register and recording the status as released along with the identifier of the person (e.g., from logon authentication) who set the status to released.

> Where relevant, a master list of persons or organizations holding controlled copies of products shall be maintained.

Distribution lists are already being maintained for quality management system documentation. These could be extended to cover distribution of product. Note that you may not need (or be able) to have full distribution control. In the case of off-the-shelf software you must rely on people registering as users to provide partial distribution control. In other cases there is no value in maintaining any form of distribution control (for example, training course handouts).

> When a product is to be changed the effect of the change(s) shall be reviewed through all possible affected items, both done before the change (e.g., product requirements and design) and applicable after the change (e.g., test plans, test specifications and testing) to ensure the change is properly integrated. Where the review shows that changes have effects on other products then these effects shall be identified and any necessary retesting defined. All affected products shall have the changes applied with the same date of effect. When the product has been changed a new version shall be created and released after all reviews, inspections and tests have been satisfactorily completed.

This calls for proper control of changes to products after release. In the case of software it is very important to have full change control and accountability through the various releases of software. Once a unit of software has been placed under configuration control formal change management procedures will need to be followed. This indicates the need for careful control over the point at which product is subject to formal control. As with corrective action it is probably best to start off with controlling the programming when it is released outside the team, for example, when it is released for user testing. In some development environments, such as the clean room, concept configuration control is initiated as soon as coding is completed.

ISSUES

Examine your quality management system and ask yourself if the following issues have been addressed and whether you can produce evidence in the form of records or documents that they have been followed in practice:

- Are there procedures for identifying the product from specifications during development, delivery, and installation?
- Is there a system to uniquely identify and record product for traceability?
- Do configuration management procedures include:
    - Version identification, issue, and control?
    - Obtaining approval to implement modifications?
    - Ensuring modifications are properly integrated through formal change control?

14

Control of Customer-Supplied Product

INTRODUCTION

This section addresses the requirements of ISO 9001–1994 Section 4.7. *Customer-supplied product* addresses the need to control and secure all customer-supplied information and material and to ensure only suitable information and material is supplied by the customer and used in the process.

If your business does not require you to make use of customer-supplied product then you need only address this requirement of ISO 9001 by a statement of this form:

> The nature of our business is such that there is no requirement to make use of customer supplied product for incorporation into the goods or services we supply to our customers.

Omitting such a statement may be construed by an assessor as an oversight or a failure to address this section of ISO 9001.

Customer-supplied product may appear in many imaginative forms, such as hat-check services, safety-deposit services, goods left for repair, dry cleaning, papers submitted for passport applications, or fixed plant or machinery that you have to go to, such as service computers, elevators, and escalators. Customer-supplied product should be properly managed, stored, secured, and maintained. Disposition of customer-supplied product should be defined. While we may initially accept the customer-supplied product, we may subsequently reject it if it is found to be unsuitable for use.

POLICIES

Typical policies addressing customer-supplied product requirements of ISO 9001 include the following:

> All product received from a customer shall be examined for suitability. The verification process shall be based on the quality management system and shall follow relevant review, inspection and testing procedures. If the customer supplied product is acceptable then it shall be recorded. Where the product is documentation for issue to more than one person, then permission to copy shall be obtained in writing, copies prepared, and distributed. While we may initially accept the customer supplied product we may subsequently reject it if it is found to be unsuitable for use.

This calls for the examination of customer-supplied product to ensure it is suitable for use or for incorporation into the products we are going to deliver to them. To preclude failure to accept because "it may not work when we get further along in the project" you should reserve the right to reject it later if it is found to be unacceptable. While customer-supplied product under ISO 9001 specifically refers to material provided for incorporation into the deliverables you should extend its coverage to all customer-supplied product including office facilities, computers, software, and operating systems and documents. Where the customer supplies documents or software there may be a need to make copies for each team member; in this case make sure you protect yourself from copyright infringement by obtaining permission in writing from the customer to make copies.

> Accepted customer supplied product shall be kept in a safe and secure manner suitable to the type of product. Our normal practices should be adequate but extra requirements may be defined in the contract. Any losses or damage to customer supplied product shall be recorded and the customer notified in writing. Any equipment supplied by the customer shall be maintained in accordance with customer requirements or manufacturer's recommended practices.

Look after things the customer gives to you and let the customer know if anything gets broken, damaged, or lost.

> If changes are received to customer supplied product, then the new or changed product shall be reviewed and accepted and the full ramifications of the receipt shall be evaluated before the product is used.

This rarely happens in most industries but frequently happens in software development. No sooner are we given some software or equipment than we are given an updated version. The requirement to manage change also extends to changes to requirements and changes to the development environment.

ISSUES

Examine your quality management system and ask yourself if the following issues have been addressed and whether you can produce evidence in the form of records or documents that they have been followed in practice:

- Is there a system for the verification of customer-supplied products?
- Is there a system to report the loss, damage, or unsuitability of customer-supplied products?
- Is there a system to safeguard and maintain customer-supplied product?
- Does the system require a register of customer-supplied products?

15

Purchasing

INTRODUCTION

This section addresses the requirements of ISO 9001–1994 Section 4.6. *Purchasing* applies to the acquisition of services, material, equipment, or subcontract products or services for incorporation into what we are going to deliver to our customer. There is no requirement to bring all general purchasing, office supplies, or equipment purchasing into the system although it would obviously make sense to do so.

If your business does not require you to purchase on behalf of your customer then you need only address this requirement of ISO 9001 by a statement of this form:

> The nature of our business is such that there is no requirement to purchase goods or services for delivery to our customers or for incorporation into the goods or services we supply to our customers.

Omitting such a statement may be construed by an assessor as an oversight or a failure to address this section of ISO 9001.

A prime point of this section is that you cannot use vendors or subcontractors as an excuse for failing to satisfy your customer's needs. You are always totally responsible for quality and totally responsible for the goods or services you acquire from other sources. There is, therefore, the need to control the selection of suppliers of goods and services and a requirement to clearly and unambiguously specify what you want to purchase. There is also the need to carefully manage any subcontractors to make sure they do not cause a failure in the quality of goods or services you deliver to your customer.

You must also be sure that you are satisfied that the goods and services you have purchased meet specification. You can do this by inspecting and testing them yourself, by witnessing inspections and tests done by your supplier, or by accepting evidence that it has passed inspection and test. The acceptance of evidence should be used only where you have complete confidence in your supplier and would usually be only from suppliers who have a certificated quality management system covering the goods or services you are acquiring from them.

Your customers may want to inspect, test, or otherwise verify that goods or services you are purchasing on their behalf meet specification. When this occurs they should make all arrangements to meet with your supplier through you. You should always participate in these inspections, first to fully serve your customers and second to make sure your customers and your supplier don't end up working directly together to your disadvantage. Be aware that you cannot use your customers' visits to your supplier as evidence that you have control of the quality of the goods or services from that supplier. Your customers cannot be held accountable if, after verifying the goods or services at your supplier's premises, they subsequently reject them. Such are the joys of doing business. If we establish all the right relationships with our suppliers, enter into long-term agreements where possible, and totally service our customers, such problems should not arise.

If you are dealing with a new supplier who has a quality management system you should review their registration certificate to make sure they are certificated to perform the work you want. You should review the supplier's quality manual and perhaps review or audit the supplier's quality management system as it applies to the work you want them to perform.

POLICIES

Typical policies addressing the purchasing requirements of ISO 9001 include the following:

> Vendors of "off the shelf" goods and services shall be selected on their ability to deliver the goods or services in a timely and efficient manner. Evidence of quality management systems should be sought. A record shall be kept of the performance of each

vendor in the vendor file. Vendor selection should be made on the basis of their historical performance at acceptable price for the grade required.

Although the first sentence appears totally self-evident, it is not what most of us do. Most purchasing concentrates solely on price, with quality and delivery almost universally ignored. It comes as no surprise to find that companies that purchase carefully have far fewer problems than the majority who buy with the motto "Cheap is best, free is better." It is good practice to encourage others to follow the quality path, so always ask potential suppliers if they are certificated to deliver what you want to buy, and if they are not certificated, when they intend to gain certification. The need to keep records means that you start your buying activities from a knowledge base rather than by relying on memory. This is especially important when many people may have the right to make purchasing decisions and we need to communicate our experiences with suppliers. Vendor selection policies may be as simple as "acceptable grade, on time at acceptable price" or may be only on the basis of established long-term relationships.

> To ensure that purchased goods and services conform to contractual requirements all items to be purchased or developed for a project shall be defined in unambiguous terms and shall be identified by suitable means to ensure that the vendor is in no doubt as to what is required. Detailed inspection and testing requirements as well as the need for special packaging, transport arrangements and delivery shall be considered. Warranty requirements shall be defined as shall the liabilities of the parties. The purchase specification shall be reviewed and approved before being issued.

The need for careful specification of purchasing becomes clear when we think of the multimillion-dollar disasters in any industry and see them being caused by suppliers who "didn't do what we wanted." The more time spent on specification the less time spent in litigation. For software developers this is especially true and applies to specification for in-house development as well as for subcontract development. IEEE 1298 has a section on the control of requirements specification and this should be carefully considered when preparing the specification for subcontract software development. The requirement to approve the purchase specification is one of only two requirements for approval (signoff) in ISO 9001 (the other is in document and data control).

Subcontractors should be certificated to relevant quality management system standards with registered capability to perform the type of work we wish to subcontract. The subcontractor's quality management system should be reviewed or audited to ensure that procedures are acceptable and being followed.

Where subcontractors are not certificated then their quality management system shall be audited to identify the degree of conformance with the specified requirements. An estimate shall be made of the extra costs likely to be incurred to ensure quality is provided to the required standard and to put a cost on the risk of using them instead of a certificated subcontractor. These additional costs shall be added to the subcontractor's bid in order to compare subcontractor proposals.

Where the subcontractor's quality management system is unacceptable then it will be necessary to either manage the subcontractor personnel who shall work to our quality management system or to provide full-time inspection at the subcontractor's premises. The cost of managing and training the subcontractor shall be added to their bid in order to compare subcontractor proposals.

A record of all subcontractor assessments shall be kept in the subcontractor's (vendor) file.

What this complicated statement says is that we want to use subcontractors who are certificated. If potential subcontractors are not certificated we should increase the allowance we make for risk (scale their bid upward) or add in the cost of totally managing their staff.

Subcontractors shall be controlled on the basis of an accepted quality plan prepared by the subcontractor and showing deliverables, review points and records to be generated. Copies of relevant subcontractor quality records shall be obtained and shall form part of our quality records. We shall require the right to review products, participate in joint reviews, witness tests and audit the subcontractor and the work on a regular basis. The detail of subcontractor control shall be defined in our quality plan for the work.

This is a very important point. One of the major benefits of ISO 9000 management systems is communication. If we and our subcontractor both run ISO 9000-based quality management systems, then the two systems should mesh together to meet the needs of the subcontract. Both parties will understand each other, and the need for quality planning, records, inspections and tests, and so forth will be understood and built into the subcontract management processes.

> Detailed inspection and testing requirements for acceptance of purchased products, goods and services shall be defined in the purchasing specification, the quality plan or the main contract and shall form part of the purchase specification. Acceptance inspection and testing shall be performed as specified.

When we buy things we must let our supplier know when it has produced what we want. This is partially done with clear purchasing specifications but may be made even more clear by providing acceptance criteria in the form of inspections and tests to be performed. You may find that the supplier already performs these inspections and tests and you may be willing to merely witness their tests or accept their inspection certificates thus significantly reducing your inward inspection costs.

> The customer has the right (if specified in the contract) to verify at our supplier's premises that purchased product conforms to requirements. This verification in no way absolves us from conformance to all the requirements of the contract or our quality management system. Despite verification the customer may subsequently reject the product. Customer verification at a subcontractor's premises shall not be used by us as evidence that the subcontractor has effective control of quality.

This clarifies the role of our customer's inspection and testing at our supplier's premises.

ISSUES

Examine your quality management system and ask yourself if the following issues have been addressed and whether you can produce evidence in the form of records or documents that they have been followed in practice:

- Does the system require a formal list of approved suppliers/contractors?
- Is there a formal procedure for the assessment and monitoring of suppliers/contractors?

- Are suitable functions required to be involved in the assessment review of subcontractors?
- Does the system require internal quality audits to include subcontractors' quality assurance systems?
- Does the system require that records be maintained of monitoring/ assessments of subcontractors?
- Does the system ensure that the purchasing documentation contains complete and precise information?
- Does the system require purchasing documents to be checked and reviewed prior to release?
- Does the system have procedures to identify the implication of customer verification requirements?

16

Handling, Storage, Packaging, Preservation, and Delivery

INTRODUCTION

This section addresses the requirements of ISO 9001–1994 Section 4.15. *Handling, storage, packaging, preservation, and delivery* addresses the areas of stock management and delivery of a product to the customer. While the wording is based on traditional physical stock control it does not take significant leaps of imagination to see how this section may be used for other issues. Some examples may be the delivery of product by electronically downloading data or programming, electronic funds transfer services, faxed messages, and airline reservations.

The objective of careful handling is to make sure that products are handled in such a way that the risk of damage is minimized. This could, therefore, include issues relating to safety in materials handling. We can even extend this to minimizing the risk of environmental damage by controlling handling of material with processes to reduce the risks of toxic spills and leaks.

The objective of careful storage is to prevent damage to or deterioration of products during storage, to make sure stored stock is regularly inspected for damage or deterioration, and to rotate stock. Obviously this can also be used to control the risk of environmental accidents by verifying that stored materials are still safe.

The objective of proper packaging and preservation is to make sure that products do not deteriorate and are not damaged in storage or transit due to inadequate or unsafe packaging. A further objective is to

107

make certain products and packaging are properly marked so that there are no mistakes in identification. This obviously extends to markings relating to hazards and handling ranging from labels such as the international "radiation hazard" symbol to the "keep dry," "this way up," and "fragile" symbols.

The objective of the delivery requirement is to make sure you identify exactly when title and responsibility passes from you to your customer and that you have suitable processes to protect the products until your responsibility for the product ends.

POLICIES

Typical policies addressing the handling, storage, packaging, preservation, and delivery requirements of ISO 9001 include the following:

> All equipment and media shall be handled and stored in accordance with the contract or the manufacturer's instructions. Where neither of these is available then due care shall be taken consistent with the nature of the product.

State the policy, and where necessary, point to the procedure to be followed for handling. If you run a computer network this section will, for example, address the processes used for message handling and accounting for transactions. Exercise your imagination to apply this part of ISO 9001 to problems you may be having with your operations.

> Product developed for a specific customer shall be stored and secured as defined in the contract or in a secure area with a process to control receipt and dispatch of the product from the secure area.

Specify the storage and preservation needs for custom-built products. Consider backup and restoration of soft products.

> Stock product shall be stored in a secured area. Stock movements (receipts from suppliers and issues to customers) shall be recorded.

Specify the control mechanisms for general stock. Consider the need for controlling user manuals and other documentation you may distribute to your end users (customers).

Product shall be packaged for stock or delivery in a controlled manner to ensure the customer receives the correct product in good condition.

Specify packaging needs.

Computer software product to be delivered to a customer shall be assembled onto the appropriate media. Media that contains software product shall be labeled with the name of the software product and its version.

We need to make sure we give the customer the software they order and verify that we have recorded it properly. Be careful that the customer cannot *unformat* a previously used disk and find something they shouldn't. Make sure you do not deliver a computer virus to your customer; this is not appreciated.

Product shall be securely packaged for delivery and clearly marked with the customer's name and address and our name and address. The contents shall be clearly marked for identification by the recipient.

Pack and wrap properly; goods arriving in poor packaging or damaged condition project a bad image.

ISSUES

Examine your quality management system and ask yourself if the following issues have been addressed and whether you can produce evidence in the form of records or documents that they have been followed in practice:

- Are procedures/instructions available detailing methods for handling, storage, packaging, preservation, and delivery of the products?
- Does the system require actions to be taken to ensure that the identity/marking of material or product is retained in accordance with specified requirements until the suppliers' responsibility ceases?
- Does the system cover product/material provided by the customer or subcontractor?
- Does the system require a secure storage area be provided with an environment to prevent any deterioration of the product?

- Do the procedures cover the authorized receipt and dispatch to and from such areas?
- Does the system require inspection of the condition of stored items to be performed on a formalized basis?
- Does the system require all shipments to be prepared and transported in conformance to specified requirements?

17

Control of Nonconforming Product

INTRODUCTION

This section addresses the requirements of ISO 9001–1994 Section 4.13. *Control of nonconforming product* addresses the need to isolate product that does not conform to specification and the actions to be taken to address the nonconformity.

Nonconforming product is any product that, having been released for integration or end use, is subsequently found not to conform to requirements. Nonconforming product may be reworked, scrapped, or a concession sought from the customer. Nonconforming product may also be regraded for another use. An example would be a watch chip that was supposed to support ten functions being regraded to go into a watch that only has five functions. Product found to be defective after installation should be reworked or replaced.

Consideration should be given to the need to identify and advise holders of nonconforming product that their product is (or could be) nonconforming. This includes such processes as national vehicle recalls for possible defect rectification.

Almost without exception, nonconforming computer software is reworked. It is, however, a characteristic of software that it can also be changed to provide different functionality. The process of changing software and reworking software is identical; because of this a single change management process should be used to accomplish both results. This provides consistency of approach to rework/change and the subsequent reviews, inspection, and testing.

There is often confusion about the difference between control of nonconforming product and corrective action. Control of nonconforming product is used for managing and rectifying product defects while corrective action analyzes the causes of defects and corrects the causes. In other words, corrective action is aimed at constantly improving our software development processes.

POLICIES

Typical policies addressing the control of nonconforming product requirements of ISO 9001 include the following:

> When any nonconformance or deficiency is identified in a product which has been released then it shall be recorded and documented in sufficient detail to enable it to be resolved.

This typically addresses the need to raise problem reports when something goes wrong. This does not mean that a complex multipage form is required. The procedure could be as simple as logging the defect onto a multiline register. Most organizations already have some form of problem/defect reporting and this should be continued. Do not redesign the process for ISO; rather use the corrective action process to drive the need for any change or improvement.

> Where physical product is nonconforming then a copy of the nonconformance notification shall be attached to the product and the product shall be physically separated from conforming product.

Most software organizations have little to do with physical products so there is no need for special procedures to cover identification and isolation (quarantining) of defective product. Sometimes we may find ourselves buying a computer on which we will load our software and deliver the package to the customer. In these situations physically attaching a copy of the problem report to the offending article is sufficient to identify its nonconforming status and prevent its use.

> Where the product is registered on a suitable register then the inspection and test status of the nonconforming product shall be updated to identify the product as nonconforming.

Earlier we looked at the use of a product register for configuration management. Here we see a further use for the register. In the case of software we may well view nonconforming product as another state in which the product can exist and assign nonconformance as a status code.

> Where appropriate, persons or organizations on the distribution list for the product which is nonconforming shall be informed that the product is nonconforming.

Where we choose to control the distribution of documentation or products then we can easily inform holders of the product that a nonconformance has arisen. Initially allow your people to exercise judgment on when to inform holders of the product. If this proves unsatisfactory, corrective action should look at providing more guidance and direction than the "where appropriate" statement above.

> The nonconforming product shall be reworked, scrapped, regraded or a concession obtained from the customer.

This is another statement of the obvious. You may need to replace this policy with some specific directions as to when each applies, but in the software sphere we traditionally rework the product (fix the bug).

> Where the nonconforming product is to be reworked then this shall be performed under formal change management processes. The need for any reviews, inspections and tests shall be included in the rework and shall ensure that all related work is also reviewed. The reworked product shall not be formally released until all required retesting or reinspections have been completed satisfactorily and authorized.

If we have invested in a system for developing product then we should apply the same controls to rework (bug fixing) as we did to the original development. Obviously, we should also be using corrective action to fix the weakness in the quality management system that allowed the nonconforming product to be produced in the first place.

> Where a managed product register is used for product it shall be updated to record changes to the inspection and test status of the product as the reworked product is reviewed, inspected and tested.

The need to track the nonconforming product through rework and back to a released product may be achieved by use of a product register.

ISSUES

Examine your quality management system and ask yourself if the following issues have been addressed and whether you can produce evidence in the form of records or documents that they have been followed in practice:

- Is there a system established and documented to ensure control of nonconforming products and documents?
- Does the system require nonconforming products to be identified, marked, and if necessary, segregated to prevent inadvertent use or installation?
- Is it defined who has the responsibility and authority to decide the disposition of nonconformance, and of external inspection and testing after repair, rework, or correction?
- Does the system have a mechanism for dealing with customer-granted concessions?
- Does the system require the recording of actions arising from the treatment of nonconformances?
- Does the system ensure that corrected or repaired products/services are reinspected?

18

Contract Reviews

INTRODUCTION

This section addresses the requirements of ISO 9001–1994 Section 4.3. This calls for us to make sure that we review any offers (proposals and tenders) we present to prospective customers, understand the contract and the requirements, and have the capacity and capability to satisfy the contract requirements. It is important to remember that a contract may be a simple order for a product or service. An example is an offer to sell you an item in a shop and your agreeing to buy it.

In its simplest sense *contract review* means that you must examine whether you have the product or service available and whether you can deliver it. If a customer wants to buy a cabbage you must ensure that you have the cabbage and can execute the sales transaction from calculating the price to packaging the product, taking the money, and issuing a receipt. At the other end of the scale we have the situation where teams of lawyers review, probe, and examine the supplier's capability to deliver and customer's capability to accept the product and/or service.

Proposals

If the proposal/tender is not prepared with the detailed consideration of the quality management system that will be used to implement it, then we stand a good chance of seriously damaging the result before we even win the work. To this end, those of us who are required to present our offer to sell in writing must do so in accordance with the requirements of our quality management system. This means that proposal/tender preparation *must* be included in our quality management system so that we start the work the way we mean to finish it. We find our proposals/tenders should be prepared in accordance with our planning processes so that whatever is sold can be delivered.

Your sales and marketing people may vigorously oppose this policy and suggest that it will drive you out of business. Which is more likely to drive you out of business: being honest and open with your prospective customers, or promising the moon and then passing the unachievable promises to the delivery people? You will find your customers will be delighted at knowing exactly what you are trying to sell them and your delivery people will be ecstatic at being able to satisfy the customer. This is a very important part of the underpromise-and-overdeliver cycle.

Your policies should, therefore, address proposal preparation/tender response, including the formal preparation of documents in accordance with defined processes, the review and approval of the documents, placing the documents under formal control, and issuing copies of the documents in a controlled manner. Policies and processes are also required for updating and changing the documents. Everyone should know what the latest version is and who holds copies of which version so that we can avoid confusion and argument about which document is the right one. This process of formal preparation, review and approval, formal signoff and issue, and formal change control is required for all documents produced. Contrary to what might be your initial belief that this will stifle the system, slow everything down, and let your competitor gain an advantage, this process will reduce wasted time, increase the likelihood of a document being produced properly the first time, increase your credibility with your customer, and generally give you a significant edge.

Once the proposal has been presented to the customer there must be processes to monitor its selling to the customer and the preparation of revisions. Should the proposal not be accepted you should declare this to be a problem and initiate corrective action to determine its cause (why did we waste time and money on a proposal/tender that the customer did not accept?) and increase our chances of getting more accepted proposals/tenders.

Contract Review

When the proposal is accepted there is the need to formally review its acceptance and ensure that what is accepted was what was proposed and that any variations between a contract and the tender are reviewed and that we can deliver what we are being asked to deliver. The results of this review must be written down as evidence that the processes of contract review were followed.

Requirements Specification

Part of the contract review process is a need to ensure the requirements of the contract are clearly understood and documented. What about contracts where one of the things we are called upon to do is specify the requirements? This is especially common in the computer systems development business where the requirements specification is the first part of the contract. This is a weakness of ISO 9001, which assumes the contract is the specification. The definition of requirements is discussed in detail under design and uses IEEE 1298 for guidance on controlling requirements specification.

POLICIES

Typical policies addressing the requirements of ISO 9001 are as follows:

Proposals

> Proposals should be prepared following the general principles of quality planning. This is to enable a smooth transition from the accepted proposal to the execution of the contract.

This is so obvious and happens so rarely that it often becomes one of the first major benefits of implementing a quality management system. It means that we start off planning to satisfy the customer by dealing with the customer and the customer's expectations in a manner that flows smoothly from the sale to the delivery.

> Proposals shall be reviewed and, if acceptable, authorized for issue by the Chief Executive Officer.

You may change who authorizes proposals, but remember that they may be betting the business. A proposal may be accepted by the customer as a contract by the customer making it an addendum to their standard terms and conditions of contract.

> Proposals are to be subject to formal distribution control. A backup shall be retained on computer readable media.

Proposals are like any other document. They may go through many versions and it is vital that control is maintained over the copies. This will minimize the risk of copies getting to competitors and enable negotiations to take place without the confusion of people referring to different versions of the proposal.

> Changes to the proposal are initiated as part of contract review.

If the customer is asking for changes to a proposal it must be assumed that some form of negotiation is now taking place and the control over this should be part of contract review.

Contract Reviews

> Formal written contracts are to be reviewed to ensure that they are fully understood and in accordance with the proposal or tender and that we have the facilities, capabilities and technical skills necessary to meet the requirements of the contract.

Contract review includes evaluating the contract, identifying areas of negotiation (including revisions to proposals), and ensuring that all issues are resolved before committing to signing the contract. Reference should be made to appropriate procedures.

> Where a formal contract does not exist then we must ensure we have the capacity and capability to meet the perceived requirements. The detailed requirements and customer responsibilities shall be documented in the quality plan.

In many cases work is undertaken based on a letter of intent or a request from the boss, but it is still necessary for you to know that you can do the job. An amazing number of people are occupied with these kinds of special jobs and the impact on resources is significant. Applying some controls should reduce wastage and lessen overload by thinking before we throw odd jobs around.

> Orders for stock products shall be checked, stock verified and delivery mechanisms verified to ensure we can satisfy the order.

In a simple order-taking situation procedures must be in place to take the order, verify product (stock) availability, and verify delivery capability. Reference should be made to order-taking procedures.

Requests for service or support shall be immediately actioned to resolve the request or the request should be handed to an appropriate person for action. Under no circumstances is a request for service to remain unactioned for more than one working day.

Servicing as a subject under ISO 9001 is usually taken to cover servicing and support of products we have delivered to our customers (maintenance). Servicing in the form of help desks, network support, and other support activities may be a business in its own right or may even be the business you wish to have certificated. In this case a request for service is a contract or an order.

Project Initiation

When a project has been accepted then the relevant manager shall be notified of the full details of the project. This notification shall include originals or copies of all relevant tenders, proposals, contracts, work papers and correspondence. A verbal briefing should also be provided.

Within software development we often find that projects are not clearly assigned and therefore not clearly managed. To resolve this issue it is useful to include a transition mechanism to let the delivery people know that a project has started and that they are now responsible for its execution. To this end a procedure is needed to formally notify the relevant delivery or development manager of the job and hand over responsibility for its delivery.

On being notified of a project the manager shall assign a project manager and a quality management representative. Other principals involved shall also be assigned. All participants and interested parties shall be notified in writing of the project and the principal participants.

The next step in initiation is to assign the project to the delivery team. The manager should be formally nominating and advising the project manager of the project. Other interested parties such as Quality Assurance will also need to be notified. The project manager should be tasked with preparing at least an initial plan as the highest-priority item.

ISSUES

Examine your quality management system and ask yourself if the following issues have been addressed and whether you can produce evidence in the form of records or documents that they have been followed in practice:

- Does a formal system exist for proposal preparation?
- Does the system provide for proposals to be reviewed by qualified personnel?
- Does the system provide for proposals to be authorized before issue?
- Does a formal system exist for review of contracts?
- Does the system ensure records are kept of contract reviews?
- Does the system allow for review of the contract by qualified persons?
- Does the system ensure:
    - The requirements are adequately defined and documented?
    - That differences between tender and contract documents are identified?
    - The capability to meet the contract is confirmed?
- Does the system ensure terminology is agreed on by both parties?
- Does the system allow for review of customers' capability to meet their side of the contract?

19

Process Control

INTRODUCTION

This section addresses the requirements of ISO 9001–1994 Section 4.9. *Process control* addresses the need to control production to ensure that quality requirements are achieved.

The processes are the activities we perform in order to produce a unit of product or provide an instance of a service. Contract review, design, and so forth are also processes that must be controlled in order to achieve the organization's objectives. Process control includes the requirement to plan the production and installation processes in order to maximize production and minimize defects. This includes the need to specify any controlled conditions in the form of methods and work instructions.

Process control also calls for monitoring and control of process and product characteristics during the production process. These may include temperature ranges, size tolerances, and defect rates. Once meaningful characteristics can be identified and measured then a whole range of statistical quality measures can be implemented based on Shewhart control charts and the work of W. Edwards Deming and others. In software development the subject of metrics is becoming increasingly important as many quality improvement programs fail to eventuate or flounder in our lack of ability to measure what we do and whether we are doing it better when we change the processes. ISO 9126 defines the terminology we should use, such as *reliability* and *maintainability*. The international SPICE project is extending the work of the Software Engineering Institute of Carnegie Mellon University in the field of process maturity measurement, and this is leading to a clearer definition of the processes (methods) to be applied and measured in quality programs. Over the next few years this attention to process improvement and measurement should start to impact the commercial world of software development.

Processes and equipment that affect quality and require verification before being performed or used should be controlled by an approval mechanism prior to the process being commenced and at selected intervals during performance of the process. Examples of these are cleanliness of food preparation areas and ensuring enclosed spaces are free of explosive gases before hot work.

A quality plan should be prepared for each project as required by Section 4.2 of ISO 9001. This plan must include information on deliverables and review points. To enforce the creation of a quality plan a project should not proceed until the quality plan has been accepted by all project participants. The plan is the basis for subsequent monitoring (process control) activity, including routine monitoring of project status, participation in key reviews within the project, and formal project audits. The planning process must systematically evaluate all anticipated project work, including special or unusual contractual requirements, documentation requirements, inspection, validation, verification and review requirements, and specific quality plan requirements.

The plan documents the practical implementation of the agreement to execute the project. It should be a comprehensive document that tries to solve any problem that may arise in the future and thus allow us to avoid confrontation and disagreements at later stages. It is far easier to examine and decide action to be taken over future events when we are in the first flush of courtship, marriage, or honeymoon than it is to try and resolve property settlements during a divorce. Consider the plan a prenuptial agreement for a project and you won't go far wrong.

The plan defines what is to be delivered (in terms of products, services, and documentation, not in terms of requirements), how the project will be performed and managed, the reviews to be performed, the costs and schedules, and who will provide which resources and facilities. The plan should also be used to agree on staff commitments and availability from all sides. A project quality plan may be sufficiently sophisticated to allow a project to achieve certification in its own right.

Finally, there is a need for standards of workmanship, which should be specified in writing or by means of samples of work already done or pictures of good and bad work. The hospitality industry, especially resorts in developing countries, make extensive use of photographs to show the standards for room makeup, table settings, and food presentation.

It is a requirement that programming standards exist, in writing, that define both recommended and prohibited practices for program design, development, testing, and integration. These standards form part of the quality management system documentation. Note that usefulness is more important than quantity. How can anybody guarantee they have taken cognizance of a fifty-page standards manual when they have been translating a specification into programming on a keyboard? Remember, the objective of standards is to achieve the functionality, including reliability and maintainability, and not to overcontrol programming.

This section of the standard also calls for the identification of special processes. These are processes that can produce defects that the testing and inspection cannot be confident of finding. These processes must be subject to regular, formal monitoring and control to make sure they are followed correctly in order to minimize the possibility of defects being produced. Records must be kept of processes and equipment that need to meet special conditions or controls (qualified processes and equipment). Records must also be maintained of qualified personnel, that is, personnel who have special training, skills, or experience that allows them to perform qualified processes. Examples are special welding and live electrical work.

In the software development business the environment used to generate programming product is part of the process that if altered may result in a change to or a requirement to change the design. Process control must be exercised over the development environment, including secure maintenance of libraries of development software; authorized backups of software under development; the identification, storage, and handling of media containing software under development; and the control of software development tools, techniques, and processes.

POLICIES

Typical policies addressing process control requirements of ISO 9001 include the following:

Quality Planning

The documentation associated with the project shall be reviewed for quality issues including the work breakdown structures to be adopted, deliverable items to be produced and any specification or contractual issues relating to quality or deliverables. The products to be developed, phases of the development methodology to be followed and other quality related issues shall be documented as a project execution strategy.

This calls for a review of all issues relating to quality and the preparation of a strategy identifying the major project issues and the approach to be adopted in executing the project including the preparation of plans. This two-step approach (strategy, then plan) provides a checkpoint between the decision on how the project will be executed and the preparation of the detailed plan. This prevents a common project management problem where the project manager decides *this project is different* and ignores the quality management system methodologies and standards when preparing the plan. The project manager then defends the plan against change (lack of time; the customer already accepts it) and the project has now taken its first leap toward a catastrophe. Experience shows that following such a procedure usually takes only a few minutes and has the long-term benefit of committing the project to the organization's approved method of working. Of course, it may expose a fundamental deficiency in the quality management system requiring new methods and standards; at least this will be recognized and their development included in the plans.

> When required by the project strategy, a project quality plan shall be prepared for completing the project. The project quality plan shall reflect the full requirements of the contract, where one exists, and shall also reflect the requirements of the project execution strategy. The project quality plan shall include design and development planning as appropriate.

A planning procedure is required. Rather than talk about project plans and quality plans, which will evoke preconceived ideas of content, refer to these plans as *project quality plans*. Included in a project quality plan is a quality plan, a project plan, and many other plans as described in Chapter 28. These plans are the first deliverable document for a project and should be as comprehensive as possible. The need for design and development planning is included to show where these requirements from ISO 9001 are addressed.

> The project quality plan shall be reviewed and approved by nominated personnel after examination for adequacy in terms of contract conditions and the quality management system.

As with any deliverable, the project quality plan must be formally reviewed and approved.

> The approved project quality plan shall be authorized by the manager and should be accepted by the customer.

The plan must be authorized as a baseline for the project and, obviously, agreed to (accepted) by the customer. Notice the use of the word *should* when referring to the customer instead of the word *shall* used in reference to staff. The reason for this is that we can demand our staff do something and take action when they don't, but we would be silly to leave ourselves open to quality management system nonconformances by demanding our customer do something they may not want to do. Dangerous but true: We often complete projects without the customer signing *anything*.

> The project quality plan is part of the quality management system documentation and shall be subject to documentation control. A backup shall be retained on computer readable media.

The procedure for distribution control of documentation is to be applied to the plan.

> At the end of each phase or group of phases managed together, and when any significant information in the plan changes, the project quality plan should be revised and updated to reflect actual results and more detailed plans for the next phase.

The plan will be updated at least at the end of each phase of development.

Process Control

> Before commencing production the version of the processes to be used shall be verified.

There is a need to baseline the quality management system elements to be used in a project. This is later extended to other items such as software. We do this because changes to baselines of any sort have the potential to seriously disrupt a project.

> Where work is being undertaken as a project then the project manager shall prepare regular reports on the status of, and progress made on each project. These reports shall include the achievement of targets, compliance with the development plan and the status of internal management milestones.

Status reporting provides evidence of process control and is part of the visibility needed to assure good project management and to provide customer and management comfort.

Software Development

A project quality plan shall be prepared which describes the methods, procedures, standards and guidelines to be adopted to achieve the quality objectives specific to the project. This plan shall also describe the means by which adherence to the plan is to be achieved. The plan shall also describe how the process of software development, including the preparation of requirements specifications and the design of the software is to be managed. The plan shall ensure that records are maintained for qualified processes, equipment and personnel.

This is an alternative policy for planning that more closely aligns to IEEE 1298 for software development. It is a little more prescriptive than the more general planning policy aligned to ISO 9001. Either policy should be acceptable.

Before commencing development the programming standards and the development environment to be used shall be documented showing the current release of each item of development (system) software to be used.

This is a more prescriptive policy defining the need to baseline standards and tools (software) to be used during development.

When a new or changed item of software support, tools, techniques, methodologies, etc., is to be used then it shall be accepted on the basis of historical performance or tested to ensure it operates correctly.

Another IEEE 1298 requirement is to make sure that any tools you use actually work. How often do we see people leap onto the next release of a development tool only to have the project severely slow down or have major rework and recovery. If you did not plan on using a new version, don't waste your time and money changing unless you are confident it will increase productivity. Extra functionality should not be an issue. If you started a project with tools that did not have the functionality you needed and had not planned on the new software release then you are a very adventurous (and foolish) project manager.

Regular backups shall be made of libraries containing software under development. All media containing backups of software under development shall be clearly labeled to enable restoration of the libraries. Media shall be handled and stored in accordance with the manufacturer's instructions.

Again we see some common-sense requirements from IEEE 1298 in the need to back up our work and make sure we can recover from loss.

Installation and Implementation

The approach to be taken for installing products on a customer's site shall be defined. This includes the installation test plan.

Here we have a policy requiring us to plan for installation and also to plan for proving the installation was successful.

The results of testing applied during installation shall be reviewed and approved by suitable authority.

After installation make sure somebody signs off that you have completed what was planned.

Implementation shall be performed as defined. The services being provided shall be regularly reviewed and any required actions initiated.

This policy calls for implementation to be performed in accordance with some defined (documented) processes and for the results of the processes to be regularly reviewed to ensure we are doing what we committed to do.

Training

Training shall be provided as defined in the contract or in the project quality plan. Persons attending training sessions should provide feedback on the quality of the course and the trainer. The trainer shall provide feedback on the persons attending the course, the materials, venue and other relevant issues.

This policy is not for training in quality management (process training) as required in Section 4.18 of ISO 9001. This policy is for the provision of training as a service. This training may be either part of implementation or it may be training as a business (the education business). The need for assessment of the quality of training provides a mechanism on which to base improvement. There should be a procedure to implement this policy.

Special Processes (Software Development)

By its very nature software cannot be fully inspected and tested prior to release of the product. As a result the process of developing software is a qualified special process and all software developers shall conform to the documented processes specified for the project. All software developers shall be qualified on the basis of skills, education, training and experience. The process of developing software shall be continuously monitored in accordance with the defined processes.

This statement is required under ISO 9001, which calls for us to qualify special processes and calls for us to maintain records of qualified processes (this policy is a suitable record), equipment (covered under the development software baselines), and personnel (covered by our training records).

Other Contractual Services

Where a contract calls for other services not defined in our quality management system then the project quality plan shall document the services required. Procedures to deliver these services shall be documented or referenced in the plan. The procedures shall be required to generate evidence that they have been followed.

This is a useful catchall (and also a requirement of IEEE 1298) that makes sure we trap any novel quality requirements and develop suitable processes to meet them. It also identifies the need for such processes to generate evidence that the process has been followed.

ISSUES

Examine your quality management system and ask yourself if the following issues have been addressed and whether you can produce evidence in the form of records or documents that they have been followed in practice:

- Is there a system to plan production, and where applicable, installation?
- Is there a requirement for the planning to specify the requirements for design/development and production/installation equipment?

- Does the system require reference to standards, quality plan, and workmanship criteria?
- Are programming standards documented?
- Do programming standards describe approved programming practices and list any prohibited practices relevant to the language being used?
- Do programming standards cover all areas such as program design, coding, program testing and inspection, integration, and program documentation?
- Are documentation product standards documented?
- Does the system require the work to be performed in a suitable, and where applicable, controlled environment?
- Does the system ensure that development takes place with equipment, software, and processes approved and suitable for that development?
- Are methodologies, work instructions, and procedures prepared to specify the manner of production and installation?
- Do the plans, methodologies, and work instructions make reference to standards, codes, and workmanship criteria where applicable?
- Does the system require methodologies, work instructions, and procedures to be systematically reviewed?
- Does the system require processes and product characteristics to be monitored during production/installation?
- Are systems in existence for monitoring and controlling special processes such as software development?
- Does the system require personnel performing work on special processes to be adequately trained and qualified?
- Does the system require records be maintained for qualified processes, equipment, and personnel?
- Does the system provide processes for the delivery of services?
- Does the system provide processes for installation and other contractual conditions?

20

Design Control

INTRODUCTION

This section addresses the requirements of ISO 9001–1994 Section 4.4. *Design* can be considered to be any process that creates a new process, service, or product. To this end, people in the software development industry recognize that programming and user documentation (including help text and operations manual) are also design; we do it only once (or should) and the result is a service in the form of a computer system that others can use in their day-to-day business operations. The importance of design can be seen in its place in the ISO 9000 series of standards. Design is the only requirement that makes the difference between ISO 9001 and ISO 9002. If you do not design your products and services then you would be looking to conform to ISO 9002 rather than ISO 9001. Only about 10 percent of companies seek ISO 9001 conformance, and this is therefore seen as some form of superachievement. Software developers do not have a choice. Design, programming, and user documentation are all ISO 9001 activities.

As reports, manuals, training materials, and documents are produced only once, they are also covered by design control. There must be standards for the preparation of documents and means of ensuring compliance with those standards. Consultants and authors will need to be cognizant of this need. Developing computer-based material, including drawings, computer-based training, and so on, is also design. Computer programming is another form of design and is subject to design control.

In this book, a three-level signoff mechanism is used. The first signoff is the review signoff or quality assurance signoff where the deliverable is approved for release to the customer for acceptance. The second signoff is acceptance by the customer or some other party on behalf of the customer. Finally, the project manager signs off the deliverable as a baseline for use in the next phase or for delivery. ISO 9001 does not require any signatures per se on design, so you should find a mechanism that suits your organization.

Requirements

One of the hardest issues we need to come to grips with in most endeavors is determining customers' needs (*requirements*). We seem to think that a good design is the solution to our problems but forget that we often fail to determine what the problem is. It comes as quite a surprise to discover that the designers of a new automobile were considered radical when they went to their potential customers and found out what they wanted to buy. The designers of a new camera were thought to have come up with a great new concept by first developing a model customer and then designing a camera for that customer. Most of us probably harbor the belief that large companies really know what their customers want. This is not so; it is actually quite common for people to produce a solution without first understanding the problem.

How do you know what the customer wants? You work with the customer to prepare a requirements specification! After all, what gives us the right to dictate an answer? We therefore come back to the fundamental determinant of quality—specifying customers' needs. It is a painful fact that most companies fail to determine customers' needs but design what they want to design and then spend huge sums of money convincing customers that they need the product.

There is a need for practical, workable processes (methods and possibly tools) to specify requirements, review the specification, and ensure the specification is understood and accepted by the customer. Requirements definition is the most misunderstood part of any endeavor. If you don't know what customers want, how can you give it to them? If you don't know what you are trying to achieve, how will you know when you have achieved it?

An important issue with specifications is that they are feasible, that is, we can actually design a product or service to satisfy the requirement. A further crucial issue is that of testability: How will we know when we have satisfied the specification? What tests will need to be passed so that we know we have finished? There is nothing more futile than embarking on a project when you have no way of knowing when you have finished! Of course, the customer may be paying for research and development with such matters as completion being left open. This is satisfactory if the commitment is open-ended on both sides. One of the major tragedies still seen regularly in the computer software industry is the fixed-price contract with no definition of completion (especially the idea of a fixed-price contract to specify the requirements). What you will get is $X of requirements, an unhappy customer, a bankrupt or disgraced supplier, or other disaster. What you *will not* get is satisfaction and what you want. Still the myth goes on, from the big accounting firms to the backyard operators, and the misery continues. Caveat emptor—you get what you pay for and every other cliché is true: Don't stint on requirements specification (either as a customer or a supplier) or you will be dissatisfied; this is a guarantee.

Design and Development Planning

Design and development planning should form part of the project quality plan and should ensure that all activities, including quality assurance (design reviews, design verification, and design validation) activities, are planned.

People assigned to perform design work should be competent to perform such work and records should be available to provide evidence of their competency. People reviewing design should also be competent to perform such reviews and again this should be evidenced. It would be unacceptable, for instance, to have a hydraulic engineer review and approve an electrical design.

Organizational and Technical Interfaces

The *project organization* should be defined as part of the quality plan. This should show the structure of the project, including the management and reporting structures. The means of communication between the development people and the customers must be described.

Design Input

It is imperative that the design process start with adequate input, and therefore a procedure is required to review the *design input*. If an agreed-on requirements specification is not available there is serious doubt as to whether the design should proceed.

There must be identification, documentation, and review of items input to the design process (e.g., requirements specification, design manuals, product/tools manuals). Design input may include prototypes, code generated by researchers, and other novel forms. Don't be constrained by convention but aim for the best design inputs to achieve your objectives.

Design Review

The design team, supported by suitable outside expertise, should review the design as it evolves. When properly managed, *design reviews* provide a valuable training mechanism as experts participate in the review process and feed their expertise to the less skilled team members. In software development the use of design reviews is the principal means by which conformance of the software product to the requirements is evaluated. Design reviews should specifically address reliability and maintainability as well as the safety of the delivered system. Design review activities should form part of the quality plan.

Design Output

The format and content of the *design output* must be defined. This may include a documentation table of contents or a definition of the computer model to be produced.

Design Verification

Design reviews are the mandated mechanism for *design verification*. However, where appropriate, the suitability of the design may be verified using other techniques as well. The techniques to be used should be defined in the quality plan. In software development, techniques for evaluating software are beginning to be developed, and include automated verification tools.

One of the significant requirements for a design is that it must conform to all relevant regulations "whether or not these have been stated in the input information." This means it is the designer's responsibility to know local laws and regulations and not the customer's responsibility to tell the designer!

Design Validation

Design validation in software is usually referred to as testing. This is the process of ensuring that what we have developed conforms to the requirements specification.

Design Changes

Once a design has been placed under configuration management there must be a formal mechanism for controlling changes. This has already been addressed in Chapters 8 and 13 (the design is part of the quality management system documentation).

POLICIES

Typical policies addressing the design control requirements of ISO 9001 include the following:

Requirements Specification

Control of requirements specification shall be documented as part of the project quality plan. The approach to defining requirements shall ensure that adequate consultation exists between ourselves and our customer to specify the requirements.

The plan should identify the methods, tools, and guidelines that should be followed to specify the requirements. If you have one methodology, then the relevant phase may be identified in this policy statement and reference to the plan removed. The methodology, tools, and guidelines should ensure that the specification phase is a consultative process. Be careful that the use of analysis tools does not destroy the consultation process.

As each major activity or change in requirements definition has been completed to the stage where it can be inspected it shall be issued for review to ensure that the requirements are feasible and can be proven to have been satisfied.

The whole specification, each section of the specification, or changes to the specification should be subject to a formal review process. The review should ensure that the specification really does specify the requirements and that we can build a system to implement the requirements and that we have sufficient information to be able to prove that we have developed a system to implement the requirements. This is one of the major issues affecting software development and comes from IEEE 1298 (it does not exist in ISO 9001). The major issues are completeness (so that we can limit specification creep) and testability (so that we can prove we have finished). Few software developers are good at specification. Most are too keen to get onto the technical design and development phases. The need to properly specify requirements is one of the greatest contributors to producing the right system and should be used by all quality practitioners as the lever to shift emphasis from technical solutions to finding out what the customer wants. We must stop building technically perfect but functionally flawed systems.

> When the original or changed requirements specifications have been completed, reviewed in their entirety and approved then they shall be provided to the customer for review to ensure the specifications reflect the requirements. The customer shall review the requirements specifications and, if satisfied, shall accept the requirements specifications.

When we are satisfied that we have addressed all the requirements, that a system can be built, and that we can prove we have built it, then we look for final confirmation of the requirements by the customer. We should not proceed until this is obtained, except where the customer agrees to write off all wasted time if the specifications are subsequently rejected.

> If the product requirements specifications are not acceptable to the customer then corrective action shall be initiated.

While at first glance it may seem a bit strict to call for corrective action if the customer does not accept the specification the first time, it is actually a very important quality issue. If the customer does not accept the specification we have wasted our time and have probably failed to involve the customer in the consultative process. We should look at our analysis techniques and make sure that the next time we do analysis we get it right the first time. Be careful that your use of tools and techniques during analysis really does include consultation with customers and does not just leave them with their heads reeling and a desire to get rid of you until the completed system is ready for them to change to what they really want. Note that ISO 9001 does not call for this level of control and you may prefer to leave corrective action as something to initiate after the release of the specification. It is your quality management system and it's up to you what improvement opportunities to take. You can always change the rules as you get better.

> The product requirements specifications shall be subject to documentation control. A backup shall be retained on computer readable media.

The requirements specification is subject to configuration management as documentation. This means keeping track of the distribution of versions of the specification. A backup is always a good idea, so state your policy here.

> Changes to the product requirements specifications after release shall be performed under formal change management processes. The changes shall be subject to a complete review of the impact of the change before being scheduled for inclusion in the next version of the requirements specifications.

Obviously, there is no point in properly controlling the original specification and then letting changes happen without control. Changes should be performed under configuration control. Reviews and signoff should be performed to the same standards applied to the original specification. Controlled release of progressive baselines enables continuous control of development rather than the anarchy of uncontrolled change.

Design and Development

> Design and development planning shall be part of the project quality plan. The plan shall also specify the use of defined design and development processes.

ISO 9001 addresses the specific need for design and development planning and this statement shows us where to find it. Some organizations have separate plans but it is usually easier to have one document that consolidates all the project planning.

> Design activity assignment as well as the organizational and technical interfaces for review and approval of design shall be specified in the project quality plan. Tasks shall be assigned to suitably skilled, trained or experienced personnel. Groups for task assignment shall be the project team, the customer quality assurance representatives and subcontractor design leaders unless otherwise specified in the project quality plan.

This statement defines the need to document the project structure (IT staff, users, and management) so that everyone involved knows where they fit in the team and what the roles and responsibilities are. The identification of the groups addresses a specific ISO 9001 requirement. The need to allocate suitably skilled staff repeats the requirement we have already seen under training and process control. You should be able to show a plan (e.g., Gantt chart) with personnel assignments. The personnel/training records should record the education, training, or experience of the personnel to perform the activities to which they are assigned. This seems at first glance to be rather trivial but it is very common to allocate warm bodies rather than skilled personnel to keep team numbers up.

> Input to design will usually be the requirements specification or the contract. Other input may be provided or used, for example specific product design manuals. All input to design shall be recorded and reviewed for suitability. A review of previous designs shall, where appropriate, form part of the review of design input.

Design input is a complex issue. Most of us think of design input as being the specification and our intellect. Behind that intellect there is a lot of other material, including books and manuals. If you want to produce a good design (this includes programming) you may want to read some books on the subject or refer to manufacturer's guidelines (e.g., *The XYZ Database Designers Guide*). These are all design inputs and listing them is part of the demonstration of your professionalism and competence. After all, if your customer sues you for a poor database design you should at least have some evidence that you tried to do the right thing by using suitable reference material. You may have a standard list of design input material. If you do, please make sure your people read it (this is called training). Design input may be in novel forms. If you have a creative genius whose output is working code then you may use their nonstandard undocumented code as input to the formal process of designing and developing a product.

> The approach to design is described in the project quality plan and shall follow documented processes previously approved as being suitable for designing the product or service.

The methodology, tools, and guidelines to be used to design, develop, and document the system should have been approved as acceptable and suitable. Your process control system should enforce them. Any changes to the methodology, tools, and guidelines should be controlled as documentation changes. Changes may be initiated by request or as a result of corrective action finding deficiencies in the methodology, tools, techniques, and guidelines.

> As each major activity in the design cycle has been completed or each design change has been processed to the stage where it can

be verified then it shall be issued for design review. The review shall ensure the design is safe, reliable and maintainable and conforms to regulatory requirements. The project manager, technical specialist, quality management representative, manager or customer may, at any time, call for a design review to be conducted outside of the schedule. The design review procedure shall include a description of the objectives of the review, an identification of the qualifications of the reviewer(s) and mechanisms for recording review results and ensuring recommendations resulting from the review are implemented. Should another form of design verification be deemed appropriate then this shall be described in the quality plan. Such verification methods may include carrying out alternative calculations or comparing this design with a similar proven design.

This specifies the need for design reviews and addresses the mechanism for initiating unscheduled reviews. This policy extends the ISO 9001 design review requirement with the requirements specified in IEEE 1298. Design reviews/verification should be applied to design, programming, and user documentation (including manuals, reports, and training materials). If you operate a training business or a consultancy, design reviews are the process by which you determine the suitability of your deliverable.

The format, content and structure of the design output shall be defined in the project quality plan. Design output shall satisfy the design input, contain or reference acceptance criteria including meeting the product requirements specifications, conform to all regulatory requirements and identify those characteristics of the product or service which are crucial to safe and proper functioning of the product or delivery of the service.

Design output may be in the form of documentation (table of contents in methodology), computer model (CASE, DFD), programming, prototype product, and so forth.

When the original or changed design has been completed, reviewed in its entirety and approved then the design should be provided to the customer's quality assurance representative or nominated authority for verification. The authority shall verify the design and, if satisfied, shall accept the design. If the design is not accepted then corrective action shall be initiated.

The design should be signed off. This is not an excuse to bully customers into signing off something they do not comprehend. If customers do not have expertise to sign off design then you should sign off (and accept responsibility) on their behalf. (This is akin to a consulting engineer signing off on behalf of a customer.)

> The design specification is subject to documentation control. A backup shall be retained on computer readable media.

The design specification is subject to configuration management as documentation. This means keeping track of the distribution of versions of the specification. A backup is always a good idea, so state your policy here.

> Programming and user documentation is subject to configuration control. A backup shall be retained on computer readable media.

Programming must be subject to configuration control. This is best applied after unit testing and programming standards reviews. The exact point at which you bring programming under configuration control will depend on circumstances. Regularly review your policy as your quality improves. You may start off only having configuration control over production libraries and progressively tighten the rules until you use a *clean room* development, which has configuration control over first-cut code. Documentation should be placed under configuration control after internal quality assurance.

> Design validation (test) specifications shall be prepared in accordance with the project quality plan or defined processes to meet the acceptance criteria. Acceptance criteria should have been specified in the product requirements specification and/or the design output.

Software design validation is usually called testing. There is no specified requirement for unit testing, system testing, integration testing, performance testing, and so on. The *only* objective is to prove that the system implements the specification (including quality issues and operational issues). Programmers would typically devise and conduct unit testing and itemize a list of the tests applied. The itemized list is reviewed after the event, and if found to be inadequate, the programmer is guided to what additional tests are required. It is then often necessary only to prove functionality to complete the design validation. Look carefully at the use of system and integration testing. Determine whether it is adding value or whether the technical people are performing acceptance testing before the customer is given the system to play with prior to being asked to accept it. Don't duplicate acceptance testing; if you are proving functionality (including performance) then you are performing acceptance testing. Design validation is about proving we have met specification—most other testing is really doing the same thing, so if we can get all of them together we can significantly reduce testing costs.

> Design validation specifications shall be inspected for adequacy in meeting the validation (test) plans or defined processes and to ensure that all specified test and acceptance criteria are included or referenced.

The validation specifications are another project deliverable and should be reviewed and signed off.

> Design validation specifications shall be formally approved and accepted. The released design validation specifications shall be subject to formal distribution control. A backup shall be kept in computer readable form.

The validation specifications should be placed under configuration control and a backup kept.

> The design validation (test) specifications shall be applied to the design in accordance with the test plan or defined processes and the results compared with the expected results. If the results are not as expected then corrective action shall be initiated.

Testing should be performed and not only should defects be rectified but the causes sought out and corrected. This may appear radical to people who accept that errors are a part of software development, but if we never identify causes we are only guessing when we initiate improvement programs.

> The results of design validation (testing) shall be formally reviewed to ensure the design has been validated.

The formal review of testing should include a statement of the form "release *aaa* of the system was tested using release *bbb* of the validation specification to prove that the system met release *ccc* of the requirements specification." If the testing was successful the development is complete. If you can separate the acceptance of the test results from the decision for the system to go live then you will have made a major breakthrough. When the system meets specification it is finished and we can compare budget with actual. The next decision is whether customers want to use the system as is or whether they want to change it before implementation. These changes are *not* part of the original system and should be shown to be extra-cost items.

> Changes to the design, programming, user documentation or design validation specifications after release shall be performed under formal change management processes. The changes shall be subject to a review of the impact of the change on other work before being scheduled for inclusion in the next version of the design. Changes shall be reviewed and approved by the authority which approved the original design, programming, user documentation or design validation specification unless agreed otherwise.

Again we need to make sure that configuration control is applied to deliverables so that we can build on a series of released baselines rather than a flood of change requests. Note that an excessive number of change requests is a symptom of poor specification and baseline signoff earlier in the project.

ISSUES

Examine your quality management system to ensure it addresses the following issues:

- Does a formal process exist for preparing requirements specifications?
- Does the specification process provide a means for consultation with the customer to resolve ambiguities, errors, and omissions?
- Does the specification process provide a means to ensure that the specification defines the requirements?
- Does the specification process provide a means to ensure that the customer accepts the specification?
- Does the specification process provide a means to analyze the requirements to ensure they are feasible and testable?
- Does a formal system exist to plan the design/development activity?

- Does the system assign the responsibility for design/development activities?
- Does the system require a review to be performed of the resources required and the skills, training, and experience of the people assigned to design/development activities?
- Does the system allow for the identification of organization and technical interfaces and the exchange of information?
- Does the system permit changes as the design/development evolves?
- Does the system provide for the design input requirements relating to the product/service to be recorded and reviewed in a formalized manner?
- Does the system allow for clarification of incomplete, ambiguous, or conflicting requirements with the originator of the requirements?
- Does the system require the final design to be documented?
- Does the system require the final design to be expressed such that deliverables can be related to the requirements specification?
- Does the system require that the design output contain or reference acceptance criteria?
- Does the system require a review of relevant statutory requirements?
- Does the system require the design to identify those characteristics that are crucial to safe and proper functioning of the product/service?
- Are design verification measures provided to ensure the deliverable meets the requirements specification, such as:
  - Design reviews?
  - Tests and demonstrations?
  - Use of alternative calculations or empirical formulas?
  - Comparison with similar or proven designs?
  - Feedback from installation, commissioning, and servicing functions?
- Is there a formal process for performing design reviews?
- Does the system require design reviews be documented?
- Is there a mechanism to identify persons who can participate in design reviews?
- Does the design review procedure include:
  - The objectives of each review?
  - Identification of review points?
  - Methods for specifying nonscheduled reviews?
  - Identification of the job functions of the reviewer(s)?
  - Provision for recording and analysis of recommendations of reviews?
  - Means to ensure recommendations are processed in a timely manner?

- Are there procedures to review programming for compliance with standards and compliance with design criteria?
- Are there procedures to review documentation product for compliance with standards and compliance with design criteria?
- Is there a formal system for reviewing programming to ensure it is comprehensible, testable, and maintainable?
- Does the system require validation that the design, programming, and user documentation conform to specified requirements?
- Do procedures state the nature and extent of design validation?
- Does the system require the preparation and approval of design validation specifications?
- Does the system require the formal review and approval of design validation?
- Are formal procedures laid down for the issue and review of design changes?
- Is there a formal system for the review, approval, and distribution of changes?

21

Inspection and Testing

INTRODUCTION

This section addresses the requirements of ISO 9001–1994 Section 4.10. *Inspection and testing* defines the requirements for inspecting and testing products and services to ensure they meet specification and comply with technical standards. ISO 9001 again shows its origins with its emphasis on the inspection of goods received from vendors and subcontractors. If you don't use vendors or subcontractors then say so and concentrate on those areas that impact your work.

Inspection and testing covers all areas including services and product. Computer software and documentation are best addressed under design validation but the policies required are also documented here. There is a requirement to specify testing, define testing processes and verify that testing was performed in accordance with the processes, and that testing was completed satisfactorily.

An important part of the inspection and testing process is final inspection. No, this does not mean that you have to devise and run a final set of tests. Final inspection requires you to verify that all the inspections, tests, reviews, approvals, acceptances, signoffs, and so on that you had planned or contractually agreed to perform have been performed and the products and services passed them as planned. The final inspection must be performed before a product is shipped or before it is released for customer use. Final inspection, therefore, suggests that appropriate reviews, inspections, and tests are planned and that they should generate records.

POLICIES

Typical policies addressing the inspection and test requirements of ISO 9001 include the following:

Product Testing

Test specifications shall be prepared in accordance with the quality plan or defined processes to meet the defined product acceptance criteria. Product acceptance criteria should have been specified in the product requirements specification and/or the design.

This calls for the preparation of test specifications, which should be designed to prove that the acceptance criteria have been satisfied. Where an external supplier is producing the product the specification should be provided to the supplier. An initial reaction to this statement in software development is "but then they will build the product to pass the test." Isn't that what we want? If the supplier has a quality management system we can use their system and their effort to prove to us that the product meets specification and save ourselves doing any inspection and testing.

Test specifications shall be inspected for adequacy in meeting the test plans or defined processes and to ensure that all specified test and acceptance criteria are included or referenced.

The test specifications are another project deliverable and should be reviewed and signed off.

Test specifications shall be formally approved and accepted. The released test specifications shall be treated as product and subject to formal distribution control.

The test specifications should be placed under configuration control.

The test specifications shall be applied to the product in accordance with the test plan or defined processes and the results compared with the expected results. If the results are not as expected then corrective action shall be initiated.

Testing should be performed and not only should defects be rectified but the causes sought out and corrected.

Changes to test specifications shall be performed under formal change management processes.

Again we need to make sure that configuration control is applied to deliverables.

Customer Inspection and Confidentiality

The customer shall have the right to inspect products and processes at our premises or our supplier's premises. The customer should make all such arrangements through us. The customer shall be required to protect the confidentiality of all information made available for examination, inspection and review.

This addresses a requirement of ISO 9001. The standard introduces the topic with "as required by the contract." It is a largely useless statement to have in a standard because we must do whatever we agree to in the contract and ISO 9001 adds no value with this statement. The major point is to make sure your policy protects you by calling on all arrangements between your customer and your supplier to include you so that you are not squeezed out of the agreement.

Purchased Goods and Services Inspection and Testing

The need for actual inspection and testing or acceptance based on supplier records shall be defined in the quality plan. Purchasing specifications for goods and services should specify the inspection and test required. When purchased goods or services are received, they shall be examined for external damage to packaging before being accepted. Any external damage shall be noted on the delivery docket. The items shall be carefully unpacked (follow any instructions provided) and inspected for physical damage. The item shall then be checked against the purchase specification. Any damage, defects, problems or discrepancies shall immediately be notified to the supplier in writing (facsimile or letter). Where the product is unacceptable then corrective action shall be initiated and the inspection report attached to the nonconforming product.

This is a straightforward statement covering inspection on receipt of goods. You may require much more sophisticated policies and procedures if you do a lot of purchasing.

Software Tools and Techniques

When software tools, techniques, methodologies, etc. are to be installed and there is no historical performance on which to base acceptance then the software shall be subject to testing to ensure it performs satisfactorily.

Do not use unproven software. Either accept it on the basis of "three months in the market with no significant adverse reports" or prove it before you use it.

Final Inspection

When all inspection and testing is complete a final inspection shall be made to verify that all tests, inspections, reviews, approvals and acceptances documented in the quality plan, defined processes and otherwise agreed have been completed, authorized and accepted.

This is an audit of the reviews, inspections, and tests to make sure that all the planned activities have been completed. This includes all signoffs, customer acceptances, and quality assurance activities. If any have been missed then go and do them before delivering the system to the customer.

ISSUES

Examine your quality management system and ask yourself if the following issues have been addressed and whether you can produce evidence in the form of records or documents that they have been followed in practice:

- Do procedures state the nature and extent of inspection (e.g., from requirements through design/development, production, and installation)?
- Does the system require verification that the product/service conforms to specified requirements?
- Does the system hold the product until conformance is verified except under positive recall?
- Do procedures ensure identification of nonconforming products/services?
- Does the system require adequate information to be provided for the inspection of the product/service and its related documentation?
- Does the system hold and identify nonconforming items (except on positive recall basis)?

- Does the system ensure that all previous inspection and tests have been performed and that the results are acceptable?
- Does a procedure exist to perform final inspection in accordance with requirements (e.g., quality plan, specification, drawing)?
- Does the system require all final inspection results to be recorded and the records authorized?
- Does the system ensure that final inspection is performed before dispatch?
- Does the system ensure that records are maintained, stating inspection results against defined acceptance criteria?

22

Inspection and Test Status

INTRODUCTION

This section addresses the requirements of ISO 9001–1994 Section 4.12. *Inspection and test status* is concerned with recording the status of review, inspection, and test of each product or batch of product at each part of the process. Each process may develop its own product or products, which undergo one or more reviews, inspections, and tests before being released to the next process.

Records should be generated by all reviews, inspections, and tests and it is necessary to know the current review, inspection, and test status of the product or batch.

Review, inspection, and test status may be marked on the product or the container in which the product or product batch is transported from one process to the next. Inspection and test status may also be recorded in a log or register, which may be kept on computer.

POLICIES

Typical policies addressing the inspection and test status requirements of ISO 9001 include the following:

> All product is subject to one or more reviews, inspections and/or tests before being submitted for acceptance and release as a product. Each review, inspection, and test generates a record

which includes the identification of the person who released the product as having passed the review, inspection or test.

Another statement of the obvious but a most useful one as it informs your people that everything must be reviewed, inspected, or tested at least once before the work is finished.

The inspection or test status of product is recorded on the product, in the inspection/test records or in a suitable register.

This points to the relevant procedure for recording the results of reviews, inspections, and tests. This is sometimes called development status. This is another use for our product register along with configuration management and control of nonconforming product.

ISSUES

Examine your quality management system and ask yourself if the following issues have been addressed and whether you can produce evidence in the form of records or documents that they have been followed in practice:

- Does the system identify the inspection and test status of the product/service by a suitable means?
- Does the system require inspection and test records to identify who released the product/service as passing inspection or test?

23

Control of Inspection, Measuring, and Test Equipment

INTRODUCTION

This section addresses the requirements of ISO 9001 1994 Section 4.11. *Inspection, measuring, and test equipment* means any equipment used for inspection, or testing. It can vary from a simple ruler to a sophisticated simulator. The objective of this section is to ensure that the equipment used is capable of performing the measurements and testing it is supposed to perform and that measurements are to the level of accuracy required.

Be very careful when documenting the requirements of this section that you do not accidentally include measuring equipment you did not intend. Statements such as "all inspection measuring and test equipment shall be calibrated" includes such things as the ruler in your desk drawer and the toy thermometer next to the air conditioning duct. Qualify your statement in a form such as "all inspection measuring and test equipment used in the production processes shall be calibrated."

Inspection measuring and test equipment may include hardware and software simulators such as power station and aircraft simulators. It is rather difficult to borrow an airplane to test a fly-by-wire computer program. Would the programmer want to do it before the software has been tested on a simulator? Similarly, anything you develop to test products also needs to be verified as being capable of performing the tests. Computer software developers will find a problem here because it means that quick-and-dirty programs written to support the testing of other programs must first be tested and proven before they can be used. The quality plan or defined processes must ensure that the suitability of inspection, measuring, and test equipment is verified at suitable intervals and the verification results recorded.

If your business does not require you to make use of inspection, measuring, and test equipment you need only address this requirement of ISO 9001 by a statement of this form:

> The nature of our business is such that there is no requirement to make use of inspection, measuring and test equipment. Should this change then either policies and procedures will be developed or the project quality plan for the project shall specify the controls to be applied.

Omitting such a statement may be construed by an assessor as an oversight or a failure to address this section of ISO 9001.

POLICIES

Typical policies addressing the inspection, measuring, and test equipment requirements of ISO 9001 include the following:

> Verification of inspection, measuring and test equipment shall be performed in accordance with documented processes designed to conduct such verification. These processes shall produce suitable evidence that the equipment is capable of demonstrating the conformance of the product to the specified requirements.

If you use equipment that needs calibrating, you need to point to a procedure that addresses calibration or proof that the equipment (including software) works.

> Calibration of inspection, measuring and test equipment shall be done by a source which provides traceability to national standards.

Physical measurement must be traceable back to national (and therefore international) standards of physical measure.

> Inspection, measuring and test equipment shall, where practicable, be visibly marked with its calibration status and a date on which it is to be re-calibrated.

Use tags or stamps to show calibration status and expiration date.

> Equipment whose calibration certificate has expired shall not be used for inspection, measuring or testing.

If the expiration date has passed you must not use the equipment until it has been recalibrated.

> Equipment which has been strained, damaged or subjected to rough treatment shall not be used for inspection, measuring or testing.

If the equipment has been subject to conditions that may invalidate the calibration, it must not be used until it has been recalibrated.

ISSUES

Examine your quality management system and ask yourself if the following issues have been addressed and whether you can produce evidence in the form of records or documents that they have been followed in practice:

- Does a system exist to register, calibrate, and maintain test and measuring equipment? This could include computer programs used to test (directly or indirectly) other programs.
- Does the system extend to hired and customer-supplied equipment?
- Are there documented procedures for different types of measuring and test equipment, including jigs and fixtures, to specify acceptable criteria, frequency of checks, and action to be taken when results are unsatisfactory?
- Does the system require calibration records to be maintained for inspection?
- Does the system assess and document the validity of previous inspection and test results when measuring and test equipment is found to be out of calibration?
- Does the system require the degree of uncertainty to be assessed against the required measurement accuracy?
- Does the system ensure that measurement uncertainty is recorded?
- Does the system require the environmental conditions to be assessed and/or controlled for calibration and inspection?
- Does the system ensure recall/calibration in good time at prescribed

intervals, or prior to use, against equipment traceable to a nationally recognized standard?

- Does the system require the measuring/test equipment be identified with a suitable indicator or approved identification record to show calibration status?
- Does the system require equipment (including software and hardware) be safeguarded to prevent adjustments that could invalidate the setting?
- Does the system require measuring and test equipment be stored and maintained under conditions ensuring accuracy and fitness for use?

24

Statistical Techniques

INTRODUCTION

This section addresses the requirements of ISO 9001–1994 Section 4.20. The *statistical techniques* referred to in ISO 9001 are the ones used to prove products are satisfactory. If you use sampling techniques rather than 100-percent inspection, the techniques you use should be statistically correct for the confidence level you need to achieve. If you test 10 percent of a product there are two things you need to know: First, is 10 percent the right sample size for the confidence you need, or would 20 percent be better, or would 5 percent be sufficient? Consult your statistician for verification. Second, the mechanism used to take the sample must be correct, otherwise you may not be getting valid results. If you take every tenth item as a 10 percent sample, your people may be tempted to make sure that every tenth item is a good one. Again, consult your statistician. As you develop your performance statistics, describe them here and identify how the data is going to be collected, analyzed, and used.

This is a contentious area because there is an increasing movement toward metrics in software development. These metrics are defined in ISO 9126 and various programs are under way to develop objective means of measuring quality. If you do full testing of your systems, you are *not* using statistical techniques in the ISO 9001 sense. If your customer accepts the system on the grounds that 10 percent has been proven to work, therefore we assume the other 90 percent works, then you are using statistical techniques.

We must assume that few if any software developers use statistical techniques to validate software. In this case, you need only address this requirement of ISO 9001 by a statement of the form:

> The nature of our process is such that software is validated by a 100% inspection and test. As such statistical techniques are not used.

Omitting such a statement may be construed by an assessor as an oversight or a failure to address this section of ISO 9001.

POLICIES

Typical policies addressing the statistical techniques requirements of ISO 9001 include the following:

> Sampling for inspection and testing shall be performed using statistically valid techniques and sample sizes to meet the confidence level required. Statistical techniques shall be subject to independent validation and verification by a suitably qualified statistician.

Make sure techniques for selecting the samples will achieve the level of confidence required to release all the product as satisfactory. Make sure you are using statistically correct techniques by having expert assessment of your techniques.

> Where deviations occur from statistical norms then corrective action shall be initiated.

Do something about deviations from the statistically established norms.

ISSUES

Examine your quality management system and ask yourself if the following issues have been addressed and whether you can produce evidence in the form of records or documents that they have been followed in practice:

- Does the system specify that the use of statistical techniques be approved for evaluating process, product, or service capabilities?
- Does the system ensure that the data from such techniques is reviewed and action taken where required?

25

Servicing and Software Maintenance

INTRODUCTION

This section addresses the requirements of ISO 9001–1994 Section 4.19. *Servicing and maintenance* deals with the support of products after they have been delivered and, if required, installed. For software it is almost a disappointment that such a large part of our effort can be addressed with so few words.

Servicing may be limited by contractual conditions or may be a business in its own right. Servicing covers the rectification of defects, work required due to normal wear and tear, and changes in functionality and performance by applying design changes.

Handling of customer complaints and the use of them to improve processes and therefore products and services should not be ignored or taken lightly. The customer is the reason for our existence as an organization and this part of the process should be one of its driving forces.

POLICIES

Typical policies addressing the servicing and software maintenance requirements of ISO 9001 include the following:

> The person responsible for supporting a product shall modify the product when requested by a customer. These modifications shall be performed under formal change management processes.

Do maintenance the same way you did the original development.

> The response to defect notification shall be in accordance with defined processes or as specified in the project quality plan. Nonconforming product controls shall be used to manage the rectification of defects.

Control the rectification of errors in the same way you did during development. Be careful of blindly following corrective action when a defect arises. In very old systems there may be no benefit in finding out that the programmers twenty years ago were ineffective—especially if one of the programmers is now the IT manager!

> Requests for assistance (help desk or response center calls) and customer complaints shall be dealt with promptly and the details recorded for future analysis in accordance with corrective action.

One of the biggest sources of information for improvement programs comes from customer feedback. Help desks, response centers, network support centers, and other customer contact points are invaluable sources of information. Make sure you have procedures to capture that information, preferably ones that don't tie your customers up in bureaucracy and paperwork.

ISSUES

Examine your quality management system and ask yourself if the following issues have been addressed and whether you can produce evidence in the form of records or documents that they have been followed in practice:

- Do procedures exist for servicing?
- Do procedures exist for verifying that servicing meets the specified requirements?
- Does a mechanism exist to feed information to design and development?
- Does the system require standards applied during maintenance be consistent with the standards and processes used during design/development and production?

PART 3

Putting ISO 9001
to Work

26

The Documentation

Quality management system documentation to meet ISO 9001 requirements may be structured in a wide variety of ways to best suit your organization. One approach that has much to recommend it is the use of a hierarchical structure. This calls for a top-level document that addresses the organization's overall approach to quality and its policies with respect to ISO 9001 and other quality-related issues. This top-level document is called a quality manual, policy manual, or company manual and provides a useful cross-reference between the external world of customers and standards and your organization's methods, procedures, processes, standards, tools, techniques, and guidelines. It also gives prospects, customers, and staff a quick, high-level understanding of your quality management system.

The quality manual then points down to the next level or levels of documentation. For example, if it is organization policy to perform formal design reviews (in accordance with ISO 9001), the quality manual states the policy:

> All completed designs shall be subject to formal design reviews. The design review shall, amongst other defined issues, ensure the design will produce a safe, reliable and maintainable product. The design review shall also verify that all regulatory requirements applicable to the design have been satisfied.

The quality manual will then refer to a process or procedure that defines the manner of conducting a design review and how such a review is evidenced.

This enables us to have a high-level document and that provides evidence of our quality management system that anyone can reference without having to plow through reams of paper and without our having to release details of our processes. The policies, by their very nature, will tend to be stable over a fairly long time, and we therefore give our organization a basic stability while leaving the processes free to be changed as frequently as necessary to achieve our desire for continuous improvement.

The next level of documentation are the methods, procedures, processes, and technical standards. Below this we may have tools, techniques, guidelines, and work instructions.

ISO 10013 provides guidance on writing quality manuals. This book is consistent with ISO 10013.

27

Quality Manual

A quality manual is usually the first documented indication a prospective customer will obtain of your approach to quality. The quality manual should set out your overall intentions and policies with regard to quality. The quality manual should follow the format of ISO 9001 unless the processes are very well structured and stable, when the quality manual should describe the process. If you decide to follow the process-structured approach you must be very careful you do not accidentally omit reference to any part of the ISO 9001 standard.

The quality manual should not contain detailed procedures. Not only would the inclusion of detailed procedures make the document clumsy, but updating would be a continuous problem. The detailed procedures (which are generally acknowledged as confidential documents) are normally made available at the point of use through procedure manuals, process specifications, standards manuals, guidelines, and work instructions.

QUALITY MANUAL CONSIDERATIONS

The quality manual covers policy matters rather than detailed procedures and work instructions. It sets out policy and organization with reference to the procedures and practices. The content of the quality manual is specifically tailored to your organization. Among organizations in similar businesses (such as hotels or software development) there will be a surprising commonality in how they address ISO 9000 with policies, although the process details will be quite different because that is what makes one organization different from another. In the early days of documentation you will even find quite a degree of process commonality within an industry as conventional wisdom is documented prior to being refined and improved by the corrective and preventive action processes.

The quality manual will typically be between forty and seventy pages. Much less than forty pages and it risks being rather cold, brief and uninformative. Much more than seventy pages and it may be starting to move into process rather than policy. You must decide what should be included and what should be excluded.

There must be a policy statement signed by the sponsor of the quality management system. This should be the chief executive officer of the organization seeking certification and may be a regional manager, divisional head, or other leading person in the management unit. The policy statement demonstrates the commitment to quality, requires staff to comply with policy, identifies where the policy and processes are documented, and calls for everyone to contribute to the ongoing development of the organization by providing opportunities for improving the processes.

Consider confidentiality issues. The quality manual has a high probability of falling into the hands of your competitors. Avoid the inclusion of confidential data and sensitive details of interest to competitors or detractors. This is another good reason for separating your policies from your processes.

The quality manual must be regularly reviewed to reflect current thinking and practices. Avoid unofficial changes and regularly reappraise the contents during management reviews.

QUALITY MANUAL—COMMON PROBLEMS

There are a number of typical problems encountered when assessing quality manuals. These often reflect lack of understanding of the need to attend to the same level of detail in the quality manual that you call for in normal processes:

- Lack of configuration management of the documentation. This includes the need to have the issue status of each page, a page-numbering system, and the identification of amendment pages.
- Lack of a policy statement on quality signed by the person in charge of the organization seeking certification.
- Conflict between the formal, working organization structure and the structure described to achieve quality objectives. This may in-

clude lack of a description on the way the organization operates and assigns responsibility and accountability. This is especially so where the organization structure does not follow conventional practice.
- Lack of cross-reference to sections of the standard(s).
- Lack of clear references from policies to the processes implementing the policies.
- Lack of a mechanism to manage change.
- Lack of attention to design verification or design reviews, and you are seeking ISO 9001 certification.
- Lack of attention to training and training records.
- Lack of attention to details on quality system audits and management reviews. This includes identifying what is to be done and who is responsible for doing it.
- Lack of deputies, especially the management representative. When nominated people go on vacation, does quality stop?

TYPICAL TABLE OF CONTENTS

The following pages illustrate the content of a quality manual. This is presented in the same sequence as the requirements of ISO 9001. Where you need a method, process, or procedure to implement a policy don't forget to refer to the method, process, or procedure or state that the method, process, or procedure will be identified in the project quality plan.

RELEASE NOTICES AND AMENDMENT RECORDS

The record authorizing the release of the manual and each of the updates. It should also identify the build status and either contain or reference the whereabouts of the distribution list for the manual.

1   MANAGEMENT RESPONSIBILITIES

    1.1   Introduction

        Introduce your organization's quality management system and explain the manual and its structure. Point people to relevant sections for more information, particularly Section 2 for the documentation structure and Section 5 for the management and distribution of the documentation.

    1.2   Policy

        Your organization's quality policy statement. This should be reproduced on letterhead and posted around the organization for everybody to see. It may also be reproduced in promotional literature.

1.3   Organization

The organizational roles and responsibilities as they relate to quality. Do not reproduce the full organization chart and hide the quality manual in organizational detail. Stick to functional roles with common quality responsibilities.

1.4   Management Review

Specify the management review policy including the need to address suitability and effectiveness of the quality management system. Include an indication of the frequency of management review.

2   QUALITY MANAGEMENT SYSTEM

2.1   Introduction

Introduce the purpose of this section, which is to describe the quality management system, the terminology used, the processes covered, and the standard(s) used as a basis.

2.2   Description of the Documentation

Describe the documentation, which makes up the system in terms of manuals, documented processes, procedures, methods, standards, and guidelines. When somebody visits your organization this section should tell them all they need to know about what documentation you use in your quality management system. It may seem like stating the obvious, but this is a characteristic of quality management: Never assume people know things—you must write them down.

2.3   Basis of the Quality Management System

Specify the standard(s) to which the system is designed to conform and the guidelines and standards used and referenced. These may include ISO 9001, ISO 9000.3, ISO 9004.2, IEEE 1298, ISO 8402, and so on.

2.4   Definitions

List the words you use in your quality management system that may not be known or may be misunderstood. You should pay particular attention to the definitions of *approve, accept,* and *authorize.*

2.5   Processes

Provide a list of the procedures, processes, and methods you have documented in your system. This gives the reader a good feel for the scope of the system and an indication of the types of processing you have implemented.

2.6 Quality Planning

In project-based work, this is better performed as part of project management. Refer to Section 9 (Process Control and Planning).

3 CONTRACT REVIEW

3.1 Introduction

Introduce the section and discuss the requirements you may have implemented in addition to contract review as called for in ISO 9001. These additional requirements may include proposal preparation, project planning, and requirements specification.

3.2 Proposal Preparation

Document your policies on proposal preparation, review, authorization, and issue.

3.3 Contract Review

Document your policies on contract review. Remember to verify the requirements and resolve differences and make sure you are capable of meeting the conditions of contract.

4 DESIGN CONTROL

4.1 Introduction

Introduce the section and discuss any special issues you may have addressed. For software developers this includes programming and technical documentation. For consultants this includes document and report preparation. For trainers this includes the preparation of training material and training aids.

4.2 Managing Requirements Specification

Document your policies on requirements specification preparation, review, authorization, and issue. Remember to reference the appropriate processes, which should include reviewing the requirements for feasibility and testability.

4.3 Design Control

Document your policies on design planning (if not covered in project planing), design input selection and review, design output documentation, design verification, and the control of design changes. Remember that design review includes the need to ensure the product will be safe, reliable, and maintainable. Also make sure design output conforms to regulatory requirements and that the acceptance criteria are stated or referenced. For software developers these policies should also reference suitable programming and documentation standards.

5   DOCUMENT AND DATA CONTROL

5.1   Introduction

Introduce the section and discuss your approach.

5.2   Document Management

Document your policies on quality management system documentation management. This includes changes to and authorization of quality system documentation as well as the distribution of copies of parts of the documentation to those who need it and the removal of obsolete documentation to avoid its accidental use.

6   PURCHASING

6.1   Introduction

Introduce your approach to purchasing goods and services on behalf of customers. If you use these policies and processes for all purchasing, explain this and any differences between customer purchasing and purchasing for in-house use. If you do not purchase on behalf of your customers, say so here to explain why the rest of the ISO requirement is not being addressed.

6.2   Assessment of Subcontractors

Specify your policy on subcontractor assessment and recording of acceptable subcontractors.

6.3   Purchasing Data

Specify your policy on purchasing specification, including reference to your purchase requisitioning and purchase-ordering processes.

6.4   Control of Subcontractors

Specify your policy on subcontractor control, including preparation of plans by the subcontractor, witnessing tests, auditing the subcontractor, and obtaining copies of subcontractor records.

6.5 Verification of Purchased Product

Specify your policies on verification of purchased product and make reference to the processes used. If you rely on your supplier's inspection records rather than doing your own inspections, this is satisfactory; just say so rather than inventing a process because you think people expect you to do internal inspection of goods received.

7 CONTROL OF CUSTOMER-SUPPLIED PRODUCT

7.1 Introduction

Introduce your approach to managing customer-supplied product that you are required to include in the deliverable product or service. If you do not receive customer-supplied material, say so here to explain why the rest of the ISO 9001 requirement is not being addressed.

7.2 Customer-Supplied Product

Document your policies on managing customer-supplied material including reviewing for acceptability, maintaining, and reporting damage.

8 PRODUCT IDENTIFICATION AND TRACEABILITY (CONFIGURATION MANAGEMENT)

8.1 Introduction

Introduce your approach to configuration management and how products are identified and version or batch numbers allocated, and how traceability back to specifications is recorded.

8.2 Product Management

Describe the allocation of identifiers and versions to your product if required. For software development, identify files, versions (such as date and time stamp), and the specifications (design and functional specification) the file addresses.

9 PROCESS CONTROL AND PLANNING

9.1 Introduction

Introduce the processes you use to produce your products or services. For software developers and consultants this will include project management issues.

9.2   Project Quality Planning

Document your policies on project quality planning and the review, authorization, and issue of the plans. Remember to reference the appropriate processes. (A discussion on project planning will be found in Chapter 28.)

9.3   Environment Management

The environment within which work is performed should be controlled when changes to the environment could affect quality. This includes a software development environment or an environment (usually computer based) supporting design.

9.4   Installation and Implementation

Specify your policies for the installation and implementation of your products. This would include delivery of training.

10   INSPECTION AND TESTING

10.1   Introduction

Introduce your approach to inspection and testing. Discuss the sort of products and services inspected or tested.

10.2   Inspection and Testing

Specify the policies for each type of product inspected or tested. Remember that products may undergo more than one inspection and/or test; for example, customer-supplied gauges may need to be inspected as customer-supplied product as well as being inspected as inspection measuring and test equipment.

10.3   Final Inspection

Specify the policy for final inspection. Remember that for software development you may need a final inspection of the work leading up to migrating the system into production and a further final inspection after the system goes live.

11   INSPECTION MEASURING AND TEST EQUIPMENT

11.1   Introduction

Introduce your approach to inspection measuring and test equipment. If you do not use any inspection measuring and test equipment, say so here to explain why the rest of the ISO 9001 requirement is not being addressed.

11.2   Calibration

Specify your policies with respect to calibration and verification of inspection, measuring, and test equipment. This should include verification of test software and specially written programs, modules, and stubs.

12 INSPECTION AND TESTING STATUS

12.1 Introduction

Describe how you record the inspection and testing status of your products and services.

13 CONTROL OF NONCONFORMING PRODUCT

13.1 Introduction

Introduce your approach to managing nonconforming product, including the general philosophies on rework, scrap, and approaching customers for concessions.

13.2 Control of Nonconforming Product

Specify your policies on the management of nonconforming product.

14 CORRECTIVE AND PREVENTIVE ACTION

14.1 Introduction

Introduce your general approach to and philosophy of continuous process improvement. Point out how this is the area of the quality management system that gives everybody an opportunity to participate in the improvement of the work, products, services, and environment. If you use a particular philosophy such as TQM or quality circles, introduce the philosophy here.

14.2 Corrective Action

Specify your policies with respect to identification of underlying causes of problems and action taken to correct them.

14.3 Preventive Action

Specify your policies with respect to preventive action, analyzing processes, and continuous improvement.

15 HANDLING, STORAGE, PACKAGING, PRESERVATION, AND DELIVERY

15.1 Introduction

Introduce your approach to the management of products, including the need for secure storage, issues and receipts, and stock rotation and inspection.

15.2 Handling

Specify your policies for handling products to prevent damage or deterioration.

15.3 Storage

Specify your policies for storage, including security, receipt and dispatch, stock rotation, and regular inspections.

15.4 Packaging

Specify your policies for packaging and marking to ensure product is adequately identified and protected during storage and delivery.

15.5 Preservation

Specify your policy on the preservation of products to prevent deterioration during storage and delivery.

15.6 Delivery

Specify your policies for delivery, including protection of products until responsibility passes from you to your customer. Specify your policies for delivery of services.

16 QUALITY RECORDS

16.1 Introduction

Introduce your approach to recordkeeping.

16.2 Quality Records

Specify your policies for records management, including how to find the index or catalogue and from there to find all other quality records. Include how to locate records dealing with issues such as management review, audit, and training.

17 INTERNAL QUALITY AUDITS

17.1 Introduction

Introduce your audit philosophy and rationale. Consider the need to reassure people about the positive, supportive role of audit rather than emphasizing the negative, judgmental, policeman role. Stress the need to audit compliance with planned arrangements (your quality management system) rather than conformance to ISO 9001.

17.2 Quality Auditing

Specify your policies for planning, conducting, and following up internal quality system audits.

18 TRAINING

18.1 Introduction

Introduce your philosophy with respect to training and skills improvement. This may include multiskilling and rights to personal development as well as technical skills improvement.

18.2 Training

Specify your policies for identifying training needs and providing training for your people.

19 SERVICING AND MAINTENANCE

19.1 Introduction

Introduce your servicing and maintenance philosophy. Discuss the provision of postcontract servicing and ongoing maintenance. This may include engineering updates and functionality changes as well as defect rectification and maintaining operational worthiness.

19.2 Maintenance and Servicing

Specify your policies on servicing and maintenance. Consider the level of control here with respect to the level of control provided during design, development, and production.

20 STATISTICAL TECHNIQUES

20.1 Introduction

Introduce your approach to statistical sampling and analysis to verify the acceptability of products. This may include the need to maximize value from destructive testing techniques.

20.2 Statistical Techniques

Specify your policies for statistical techniques and the selection and verification of sampling techniques, measurements, and analyses.

28

Project Quality Plans

INTRODUCTION

The quality plan described here includes the ISO 9001 requirements for quality planning, design and development planning, production planning, and test planning. It also addresses IEEE 1298 requirements for project planning as well as the planning requirements of ISO 9000.3. The quality plan for a project is actually the quality management system for that project. It defines which policies are to be followed, when, and by whom. In a project organization a quality plan is required to supplement the quality manual, which often has to refer to the quality plan for the methods, processes, and standards to be used in specific projects. The use of a quality plan is a simple and straightforward way to implement totally flexible quality management systems.

A quality plan must be created for every project and should be updated for each phase. The quality plan is the basis for subsequent monitoring activity, including routine monitoring of project status, participation in key reviews within the project, and formal project audits. The planning process must systematically evaluate all anticipated project work, including deliverables, special or unusual contractual requirements, documentation requirements, inspection, validation, verification and review requirements, and specific quality plan requirements.

The quality plan documents the practical implementation of the contract or agreement. It should be a comprehensive document that attempts to solve any problem that may arise and thus precludes confrontation and disagreements at later stages. The quality plan defines what is to be delivered (in terms of products and services, not in terms of requirements), how the processes will be performed and managed, the reviews to be performed, the costs and schedules, and who will provide what resources and facilities. The quality plan should also be used to agree on customer commitments. In its best form, a quality plan should be all that is needed by both parties to satisfactorily manage a project. As the quality plan is the interpretation and application of the quality manual for a project, the wording used should be similar to that used in the quality manual. For example:

> The design shall be performed in accordance with the APT Methodology. The output from each design activity and the completed design shall be reviewed by a design review team in accordance with the design review procedure.

TYPICAL TABLE OF CONTENTS

This section introduces the major sections and then the table of contents of each section of a typical/project quality (project execution) plan.

RELEASE NOTICES AND AMENDMENT RECORDS

This page contains the signatures that approve, accept, and authorize the quality plan. It should also contain a list of each section of the manual and its version number. This enables people to quickly check if their plan is up to date. It may also include the distribution list.

1 INTRODUCTION

This section provides background information and leads into the quality plan. Write a brief description of the project, identifying the customer and the background to the project in terms of tenders, contracts, purchase order number, internal account number, and location of the various documents.

Define the scope and boundaries of the project. State what the project is going to cover and also what is not to be included. Identify the customer departments affected and how they will participate. Describe the boundaries between users, management, and teams as well as any systems and processes with which the project may have to interface.

Specify the words used in the plan that may be subject to misinterpretation. This may be a larger list than you think, as one person's *accept* is another person's *approve*. Do not fall into the trap of assuming we all use words the same way. This is especially so when you move from country to country, or even from state to state or province to province. The most important words to consider are *approve, accept,* and *authorize*. A list of commonly used words and suggested definitions are included in Appendix A.

The contents of Section 1 of the plan should include the following:

1.1 Project Description

A brief description of the project, the customer, the origins of the project (tender number, correspondence, etc).

1.2 Scope and Boundaries

Specify and document the project scope.

State what the project will do and what it will not do.

Show which departments are affected and how.

Describe the boundaries between various computer systems, users, management, and teams.

1.3 Definitions

Words and phrases that may not be fully understood by all parties. For example: *approve, accept, authorize*.

2 MANAGEMENT PLAN

This section describes the management of the project, including the organizational and technical interfaces between the groups (see ISO 9001 Section 4.4) involved in the project. In most projects the organization interface is the steering committee. The technical interface is between the project manager and the customer's quality assurance representative. Project-related information should be documented and transmitted between the project manager and the customer quality assurance representative.

A major issue to be addressed in the management plan is the political environment both in your organization and the customer's organization. This means that you must determine who sets technical standards, who has the right of veto over the project deliverables (there may be many of these), who accepts the project deliverables, and any record this person may have for prevaricating or refusing to sign off even when satisfied. Other issues include who holds the purse strings, who is the sponsor or champion, and who is the main customer. If these are different people, you may have to allow extra time and effort to coordinate between them. Also look for who is likely to support the project and who is likely to oppose it. Finally, look at what competing demands there are for resources.

Next we need to identify and record project management information. We must identify the project manager and his or her reporting structure for project and nonproject activities. We must identify the person responsible for managing quality assurance and ensuring independent review occurs as required. This person provides an alternate path for communication should delivery, political, and management issues threaten to derail or compromise the project. We also need to identify our customers' quality assurance representatives and to whom they report. The quality assurance representative is the project manager's opposite number in the customer's organization and is responsible for ensuring the customer's requirements are defined, answering questions, approving proposals, making sure the customer observes agreements made, defining acceptance criteria, and dealing with customer-supplied product that is unsuitable for use.

We need to identify the composition of the steering committee or project management committee as well as its roles and responsibilities, frequency of meeting, and secretarial arrangements. Typically, the steering committee is responsible for monitoring the progress of the project, recognizing the achievement of milestones, resolving problems external to the control or influence of the project team, and providing policy input to the project. Wherever possible, the project manager should be responsible for secretarial; this way the minutes will reflect the project manager's understanding of what was agreed. As this is what will be done, it is best if the other members of the committee are aware of any differences in understanding.

The need for any technical or operational working parties should be identified along with their composition, roles and responsibilities, decision-making powers or limits, and secretarial and meeting arrangements. Working parties should be established and meet as required to resolve technical and operational issues. The members should have the right to make decisions and commitments affecting their area of operation.

Consider the role of customer's staff in the project. Customer's staff will be involved in the project in various roles during specification, documentation, and testing. They are team members and should have tasks allocated to them and be monitored against these. Failure by users to complete tasks or to complete them on time is a common cause of project slippage. You must hold them accountable as they have a significant responsibility for the quality and timeliness of the resulting system. Customers should (with appropriate assistance) participate in requirements specification, specify acceptance criteria, produce acceptance test specification, participate in acceptance testing, and log any problems encountered or changes requested.

Specify the requirements for status reporting, including the frequency of status reporting, the process to be followed, the format in which status reports are to be presented, and the distribution list of recipients of the reports.

Specify the process of resolving issues by communication between the project manager and the customer's quality assurance representative. This includes the requirement to resolve issues in a timely manner.

Identify the project risks including failure to deliver, delays caused by ourselves or the customer, and schedule problems caused by resources not being available as planned. A significant risk factor is failure to complete assigned tasks to the agreed schedule, typically customer delays in accepting intermediate deliverables or specifications.

Specify the actions to take place when identified risks eventuate. These may include penalties, accepted schedule slippage, project scope and functionality changes, or even project cancellation. Insistence on planning for these eventualities will often result in unrealistically dictated deadlines evaporating and the job of scheduling being left to the project manager instead of being specified by the customer. Typical statements include the following:

> In the event of the project suffering slippage of greater than one month then the functionality to be implemented in the first release shall be reviewed by the quality assurance representative and the project manager and a revised set of functionality defined and agreed with the user representative.
>
> All customer review and acceptances shall be completed within ten working days of the product being handed to them. Should any customer agreed review period not be met and, in the opinion of the project manager, the project is unable to proceed then the team shall be paid at the agreed rates until they are able to recommence. The schedule shall be adjusted by the time lost.
>
> Should any customer agreed resources not be made available as scheduled in the plan and, in the opinion of the project manager, the project cannot proceed then the team shall be

paid at the agreed rates until they are able to recommence. The schedule shall be adjusted by the time lost.

Specify who provides the facilities from office space to design, development, test, and installation equipment.

Specify what material and information is to be supplied by the customer. Specify when it is to be supplied and how it is to be reviewed, inspected, and tested for suitability. Explain how customer-supplied material will be accounted for, stored, and maintained. Specify the process for reporting lost, damaged, or unsuitable product to the customer's quality assurance representative.

Specify the skills the team members need to perform their tasks and the equipment and other resources required to support them. This includes the customer's staff where they are participating in the project. Training needs must be identified and necessary training planned as part of the quality plan. Also consider on-the-job training and skills transfer and the impact of these on the project.

Specify the process to be followed for requesting and processing changes. These should refer to your standard change request procedures. Explain the need for changes to be formally processed from specification changes through all design/development, production, inspection, testing, and installation. This explanation will be found useful in educating the customer to the ramification of changes and in obtaining suitable funding and schedule to perform the changes properly.

Specify the process for reporting problems and the effect of problem resolution through rework, scrap, or concession as well as the corrective-action approach to resolve and rectify the cause of the problem. This demonstrates your approach to quality and will help in enlisting the customer's support for your approach to quality.

Include a confidentiality statement in the quality plan if one has not been agreed on as a part of the contract. Both parties should respect the confidentiality of each other's business methods, technology, and processes. A typical statement may be:

> Both parties and their staff, agents, contractors and subcontractors shall respect the confidentiality of each other's business and technology and shall not reveal any information concerning the other party without the written permission of the other party.

Specify the requirement for joint reviews of the project and/or the project management process. This includes the need to conduct quality management system audits. The methods for requesting and conducting such reviews should be detailed.

Specify the process to be followed for updating the quality plan. This will include specific events that will trigger a plan update, such as changes to technology and completion of phases. The general philosophy of updating to keep the quality plan relevant should be documented. The process should include managing the progress of the updated plan through acceptance by both parties. The day-to-day cost and schedule data should be maintained outside of the quality plan to reduce the frequency of change. The quality plan should contain only the broad phase plans with accepted initial plans, accepted major revisions, and the actual results. There should be a requirement to update the plan with the final actual results at the end of the project. This will provide a valuable record and information for future project planners.

2.1   Management

    2.1.1   Project Management

        Who is the project manager and to whom do they report?

        Who is the (lead) quality inspector and to whom do they report?

        Who is the customer's quality assurance representative and what are their roles and responsibilities?

        What are the organizational and technical interfaces between the groups? (The usual groups are the project team and the customer.)

    2.1.2   Steering Committee

        What is the composition of the steering committee?

        What are its roles and responsibilities?

        How often does it meet?

        Who is the secretary (usually the project manager)?

    2.1.3   Working Party

        A working party is the usual form of technical interface between the project team and the customer's technical organization.

        Are there any working parties?

What are their roles and responsibilities?

How do they meet, who attends, who chairs, and who is secretary?

2.2   Status Reporting

What is the frequency of status reporting?

How is it done?

2.3   Risk Management

How are issues to be managed to ensure they are resolved?

What are the risk areas?

What is to be done if identified risk factors come into play?

What contingencies are there?

Typical risks are:

Failure to deliver.
Customer caused delays.
Supplier caused delays.
Unavailability of resources.

2.4   Provision of Facilities

Who is providing development facilities?

Who is providing test facilities?

2.5   Customer-Supplied Material

What information and material is the customer going to provide?

When will this material be provided?

How will it be reviewed for acceptability?

2.6   Skills and Resource Requirements

2.6.1   Skills and Resources

What resources are required and what skills do they need?

2.6.2   Training

What training is required in order to meet contract requirements?

Procedures, methods, and standards.
Quality assurance skills.
Technical skills.
How is the training to be provided?

Is any skills transfer required?

2.7   Changes

How are changes requested and processed?

2.8   Problems

How are problems reported and managed?

2.9   Confidentiality

Use a standard statement on confidentiality.

2.10   Joint Reviews

Are joint project and/or project management reviews required?

How will they be conducted, who will attend, who will be secretary?

2.11   Audit

Will the customer be auditing the project? How? When?

2.12   Updating This Plan

The plan will be updated at the end of each phase, at the end of the project, and at other times as deemed necessary.

3   QUALITY PLAN

Specify the quality management system documentation components to be used for the project. This includes the procedures, processes, methods, standards, tools, techniques, guidelines, and work instructions to be used during the execution of the project. These may even be supplied by the customer. It is by specifying this information for each project and making provision for the project to develop and use its own unique standards that we can end up with a totally flexible quality management system that can be quickly tailored for each project. This is because the quality plan for the project is defined (in the quality manual) as part of the quality management system.

Specify the processes to be followed if quality management system components change as well as the process for retaining copies of the quality management system documentation as records of the projects. The processes should cover all project phases, including requirements specification; design/development; production; inspection and test; installation and implementation; and maintenance and servicing.

The design/development and process environments must be specified and processes specified for managing changes to these environments. In software development projects provision should be made for generating and managing backups of software and soft copies of documents.

The project manager should document each tool, document, and product that constitutes the environment in which the system will be designed/developed and produced. This includes the versions of the products and documents (including standards manuals). If *any* of these change, the impact of the change should be analyzed and the cost and schedule for the project adjusted. Problem-reporting processes should be used for this.

Specify any tools or equipment to be used for inspection, testing, validation, and verification of design/development or products/services. Specify the processes to be followed to calibrate or verify that these products are capable of performing the tests required.

Describe the design/development and production/delivery cycle to be followed by the project in terms of processes, procedures, methods, and work instructions.

Specify what products are to be developed by the project including any intermediate specifications. These products may include this quality plan, requirements specifications, design documentations, products (including computer programs and user documentation), services, and test specifications.

Summarize the reviews, acceptances, inspections, and tests that must be done before handing a project deliverable to the customer for use. These must be checked for completeness (final inspection) before you formally hand over the product to the customer even though the customer may have been using the product for verification and validation purposes.

Specify what records are to be kept and the processes to be used for collecting and keeping them. Remember to include the collection and retention of subcontractor records. Also specify what records are to be copied to the customer. Identify the retention requirements for the records, including the access requirements of the customer.

3.1   Development Standards

Specify the documentation (quality management system processes, procedures, methods, standards, guidelines, tools, and techniques) to be used. Include versions.

How are changes to documentation progressed?

What requirement is there for the retention of superseded versions of standards and procedures?

3.2   Development Environment

Specify the development environment.

How are changes to the development environment handled?

3.3   Inspection, Measuring, and Test Equipment

Describe any special tools, techniques, inspection, measuring, and test equipment that needs to be acquired or developed for verifying the project deliverables or the process of developing those deliverables.

How will the equipment be verified?

3.4   Development Cycle

What phases from the methodology will be used in this project or what life cycle will it follow?

3.5   Products to be Developed

What products are going to be developed?

> Project quality plan.
> Consulting reports.
> Requirements specification.
> Design documentation.
> User documentation.
> Programming.
> Test specifications.
> Other.

3.6   Final Inspection

Summarize the acceptances that must be done before handing the product or intermediate product to the customer.

3.7   Records

What records are to be kept, and how?

What records does the customer require?

For how long does the customer want access?

How long does the customer want us to keep them?

How long are you going to keep the records?

4   PURCHASING PLAN

Specify what is to be purchased for the project. Make sure you reference the contracted requirements to ensure purchasing conforms to the customer's requirements. Identify any subcontract purchasing. Specify the processes to be followed for selecting suppliers. Suppliers should be selected on the basis of their historical performance at acceptable price for the quality required. The register of approved suppliers should be examined before initiating purchasing action. Look for evidence of quality management systems and certification to provide the goods and services you require. Specify what is to be purchased in sufficient detail to ensure your customer gets the goods and services specified in the contract between you and your customer. Detailed inspection and testing requirements as well as the need for special packaging, transport arrangements, and delivery should be considered. Warranty requirements should be defined as should the liabilities of the parties. The purchase specification should be reviewed and approved before being issued.

If you are using subcontractors, then you will need to specify how subcontractors are to be controlled. If your subcontractor has a certificated quality management system then you should control your subcontractor on the basis of a quality plan similar to this plan, with the subcontractor plan being back-to-back with your plan for delivering the project to your customer. If your subcontractor does not have a suitable quality management system you will need to work together to develop a suitable plan or put sufficient inspection and test people as well as quality assurance representative time into ensuring your obligations to your customer are met. Subcontractor control should also include documented agreement on joint reviews, participation in testing, witnessing of tests, auditing of your subcontractors, and provision of copies of records by your subcontractor to become part of your records for the project.

Specify the processes to be followed to inspect and test purchased goods and services to ensure that they conform to the specified requirements. This includes any requirement for your customer to verify at your supplier's premises that the goods or services conform to requirements. If your customer has elected to do this, be sure that all such arrangements are made between your project manager and your customer's quality assurance representative. Remember that this verification in no way absolves you from conforming to all the requirements of the contract or your quality management system.

Detailed inspection and testing requirements for acceptance of purchased products, goods, and services should have been defined in the purchasing specification, this quality plan, or the main contract. This detailed inspection and testing should form part of the purchase specification to your supplier or part of the contract with your subcontractor.

4.1   Purchasing Requirements

What has to be purchased?

Does this include subcontract development?

4.1   Selection of Suppliers/Subcontractors

How to select suitable vendors.

4.2   Purchasing Specification

Specify the purchasing requirement and how is it to be inspected.

4.3   Subcontractor Control

How are we going to control subcontractors?

Use an acceptable project quality plan developed by the subcontractor.
Joint reviews, witnessing of tests, audits.
What records do we want from the subcontractor?
Organizational and technical interfaces with subcontractors.

4.4   Verification of Purchased Product

How are we going to verify purchased product?

What about customer verification and access to subcontractor site, vendor site, or our site?

Subcontractor control.

5   DEVELOPMENT PLAN

The development plan should specify the processes to be followed to produce this project quality plan, review it for correctness and suitability, and have it accepted by your customer before being issued as a baseline for the project. The processes defined should include the mechanism for changing and updating this project quality plan as required.

The processes for generating the requirements specification should be defined, including the processes for reviewing the requirements for feasibility and testability, for ensuring the requirements specification is accepted by the customer and for changing the requirements specification if needed. The people involved in requirements specification (particularly your customer's people) should be identified and their commitment defined.

The processes for design/development should be specified, including the design verification mechanisms, design review process, and the design validation process. The design process should include reviewing information input to the design process; defining the format of the design output, including referencing or containing the acceptance criteria; and approval of the design and any changes by a suitable person or organization. Processes for design changes should be identified. Documents in the form of manuals, consultancy reports, and training material are also design output, as is computer programming. These should all be subject to your design control processes. Identify the people involved in the design and how design information is communicated between different groups of people as appropriate. This may include joint reviews, working parties, computer networks and electronic mailing, or plain mail and facsimile.

The processes for producing the products or services and the necessary controls should be defined. This should also include the need to control and monitor the process rather than the products, where the products cannot be assured as being defect-free on delivery. The installation and implementation processes should also be specified as appropriate.

5.1   Project Quality Plan (This document)

    5.1.1   Organization and Staffing
        Staff allocated to planning.

    5.1.2   Project Planning
        How it will be done (procedures/methodology).
        Activities (usually only detailed in the phase plan).
        Standards and guidelines to be adhered to.
        Allocation of tasks to people.

    5.1.3   Review of Project Plan
        Who will review?
        Viability and achievability.

    5.1.4   Acceptance of Project Plan
        Quality inspector approve.
        Did the customer have opportunity to contribute?
        Customer acceptance.

    5.1.5   Issue Project Plan
        Project manager authorize.

    5.1.6   Changing Project Plan
        Change request.

5.2   Functional Requirements

    5.2.1   Organization and Staffing
        Skills required and, if known, staff allocated to requirements.

Customer staff and committed availability.

Management of staff, including customer.

5.2.2   Requirements Specification

How it will be done (methodology and phases)?

Activities (usually only detailed in the phase plan)

Standards and guidelines to be adhered to.

Allocation of tasks to people.

5.2.3   Review of Requirements Specification

Who will review?

Feasible and testable?

5.2.4   Acceptance of Requirements Specification

Quality inspector approve.

Did the customer have opportunity to correct any ambiguities, errors, and omissions?

Does the specification reflect the requirements?

Customer acceptance.

5.2.5   Issue Requirements Specification

Project manager authorize.

5.2.6   Changing Requirements Specification

Change request.

5.3   Design

5.3.1   Organization and Staffing

Skills required and, if known, staff allocated.

Customer staff and committed availability.

Management of staff, including customer.

5.3.2   Design Input Register and Review

Review design input and register.

5.3.3   Design

How it will be done (methodology and phase).

Activities (usually only detailed in the phase plan)

Allocation of tasks to suitably skilled staff.

Standards and guidelines to be adhered to.

5.3.4   Design Output

How specified (methodology).

5.3.4   Design Review

Review points (activities).

How to specify nonscheduled reviews.

Who will review?

Acceptance criteria shall be promulgated from requirements.

Safe, reliable, maintainable?

5.3.5   Acceptance of Design

Quality inspector approve.

Will the customer accept or the project manager?

5.3.6   Issue Design

Project manager authorize.

5.3.7   Changing Design

Change request.

Approval by authority that approved original design or acceptable alternative.

5.4   Programming, documentation product, test specifications, and so on.

Follow the above pattern.

6   TEST PLAN

Specify the inspections and testing required for design validation and the processes to be used to conduct them. The test plans should include the participation of your people, your customer's people, and any other organization such as independent validation and verification organizations or regulatory authorities. Also identify any test facilities as well as special testing tools and equipment. The acceptance criteria contained or referenced in the design/development documentation should be specified and processes defined for how this information is to be used in the testing.

The test plans should include definitions for various levels of testing where, for instance, products have to be tested in isolation before being assembled for integration testing and finally being subjected to formal acceptance testing prior to being handed over to your customer. Remember to control the versions of product being tested against versions of test specifications being used to prove conformance with versions of the requirements specification.

6.1 Facilities and Tools

What test facilities are required and who is providing them?

Are any special testing tools or equipment required?

6.2 Acceptance Criteria

Acceptance criteria shall be promulgated from design and requirements.

6.3 Unit Testing

What is to be done, and how?

How is it to be documented?

6.4 System and Integration Testing

What is to be done?

Subsystems, integration with hardware, or other systems?

What is the approach and what documentation is required?

6.4 Acceptance Testing

Who does it, and how?

Are test specifications to be produced; by whom?

How is testing to be conducted?

Review test results.

Certify test completion.

7 INSTALLATION, IMPLEMENTATION, AND DELIVERY PLAN

7.1 Installation

What is required?

Do any special procedures have to be written?

Who does what?

7.2 Implementation

Follow the pattern in the development plan.

7.3 Handling, Storage, Packaging, Preservation, and Delivery

Are there any special requirements to be addressed?

7.4 Other Contractual Services

Are there any other contractual services to be provided?

How will they be provided?

8 PRODUCT MANAGEMENT PLAN

Specify how product will be managed in terms of identification and traceability of individual products or batches of products back to the specification. Complex products, including computer software, should have the configuration management processes and tools specified. Specify how the records will be managed, products identified, and version numbers allocated and controlled, and how products will be isolated and secured as they pass through various stages of inspection and test. This control should include the processes for controlling nonconforming product.

8.1   Product Register

What information will you keep on the product register?

Will it be computerized?

8.2   Product Identification

What types of products will you be developing and how will you identify them?

What filenaming conventions will you use?

8.3   Version Control

What type of version control will you use?

How will versions be allocated? (May be computer generated such as date and time stamps.)

8.4   Maintenance of Libraries

How will files be migrated between libraries?

What backups will be kept, and where will they be kept?

8.5   Nonconforming Product

Will you be isolating nonconforming product? How?

Review and disposition of nonconforming product.

9   MAINTENANCE PLAN

Specify the maintenance period, what days and times maintenance will be provided, and how your customer will request maintenance. Maintenance processes should be specified and should have the same extent and depth of control that was applied during the development of the product.

9.1   Maintenance

What is the warranty or maintenance period?

What days and times will maintenance calls be accepted?

How does customer contact us—phone numbers and/or fax numbers?

How will functionality changes be requested and managed?

How will customer be notified of defects and defect rectification managed?

How will requests for help/support be managed?

10 THE PROJECT PLAN

Prepare estimates of costs and schedule in as much detail as possible with the information at hand. Where a project consists of many phases, the first phase may be fixed price or a time and materials estimate that we would expect to be within 10 to 15 percent of the end result. Forecasts may be prepared for subsequent phases, but the fact that they are a forecast must be highlighted. The plan would normally be in the form of a chart supplemented by data on costs and resource requirements. Detailed day-to-day operating plans should be kept external to this plan to avoid too frequent changes to this plan. This plan should contain only the broad phase plans. Update this plan at least at the end of each phase and at the end of the project.

This is a *traditional* project plan using Gantt charts, project management tools, and so forth. Detailed working schedules should be provided as an appendix to reduce the number of updates to this plan; however don't fall too far out of synchronization before updating this plan. The working schedules must show who is assigned to what activity in order to satisfy the need for design and development planning.

10.1 Overall Project Plan

10.2 Functional Requirements Phase Plan

> 10.2.1 Plan
>
> 10.2.2 Milestones and Payment Schedule
>
> 10.2.3 Actual
>
> > Other Phase Plans (for example, design, programming, testing, installation)

29

Process Documentation

INTRODUCTION

Process documentation includes procedures, methods, work instructions, standards, and guidelines. The process documentation must be designed to ensure the work that has to be done is done in such a way that quality objectives are achieved. There is a tendency in process documentation to go for quantity rather than quality. Part of the problem is the desire to specify the process down to every last detail and assume this will produce the desired results. While some processes may need this level of detail, others will only require a properly designed form to achieve their objectives. You must make sure your process documentation is suitable for the end user. Too much detail for professional persons will not only insult their intelligence but may also compromise their right to use their own judgment. (And this may be the very ingredient you need in your process.) Too little detail, on the other hand, may leave your people unsure of what to do and how to do it. Aim your process documentation to the level you and your documentation team feel is best and then let corrective action and audit refine the processes. If in doubt, write less rather than more. It is easy to use corrective and preventive action to tighten up processes but very difficult to identify opportunities to reduce the amount of documentation.

Process documentation may use any medium you feel is appropriate in getting the message across. This is the only contact many people have with the rest of the organization and must therefore be seen as representing the organization to its people. When you consider the difference in cost between getting a customer in the door and recruiting an employee, it comes as a great surprise that the customer is wooed with the finest professionally produced information from a variety of media and the employee is treated to a dog-eared copy of a photocopied photocopy. If that is the way you treat your people, they will probably return the compliment and treat their process with carelessness.

It is important to remember that the processes describe *how* you run your organization and, as such, are probably sensitive and confidential. After all, they represent the accumulated knowledge and skills gained in the improvement of your processes and it would be ridiculous to let this accumulated wisdom fall into the hands of your competitor. Keep them confidential.

The process documentation should also contain roadmaps to describe what processes must be followed when. These roadmaps will cover the standard set of procedures required for routine work as well as pointers to relevant procedures to follow when an event occurs (such as a problem being identified).

One of the requirements of processes is that they should produce evidence that the process has been followed. The evidence may be a product or a record. The evidence should be available to show your customer or an external assessor that a satisfactory quality system is in place and operating. Real evidence of quality must be seen to exist, not only in the completed system, but in all processes that lead to the final deliverable. By controlling all of these processes in a systematic manner you can be reasonably assured that each process was performed correctly before the next process was started.

The development of formally documented processes brings a number of benefits. This includes taking the time to think through what has to be done, who should do it, why it should be done, the time scale involved, and how it must be done. Documented processes can be critically reviewed in order to optimize productivity and quality. Clear instructions are an invaluable aid to communication and training throughout the organization and also with customers and suppliers. Documented processes provide a firm base from which to introduce changes as well as providing a mechanism to investigate possible causes of problems. Process documentation should be formally reviewed at least once a year to determine that it is still suitable and relevant. This review should be conducted even if the process has been changed during the year; quite often, changes do not include a review of the whole process or its relationship to other processes. Process documentation should generally contain the following sections:

- PURPOSE
  This section shall clearly and concisely explain the specific aim(s) of the process.
- SCOPE
  This section defines the coverage of the process in terms of what is covered (and not covered) by the process.
- DEFINITIONS
  Words and terms used in the process that may cause confusion shall be defined or reference made to relevant documents.
- REFERENCES
  Bibliography of Standards and other documents referenced in the process.
- RESPONSIBILITIES
  Defines who is responsible for what. This specifically includes who does the work (follows the process), who reviews the work (if required), and who approves the work as being completed.
- PROCESS
  Describes how the work (executing the process) is to be done. The description may range from little more than support on how to fill out a form to a detailed set of work instructions, flowcharts, and so forth.
- RECORDS
  Describes which records or forms are used and retained to prove that the process has been followed.

PREPARATION OF PROCEDURES

The following procedure will provide you with a starting point. It is a procedure for writing procedures. Use it as a base to decide how you want your procedures to look, how you want them written, and how you want them approved.

1 PREPARATION OF PROCEDURES   QP0350

    1.1   PURPOSE

         This procedure describes how quality management system procedures are to be developed and maintained.

    1.2   SCOPE

         This procedure shall be followed when preparing or modifying any quality management system procedure.

    1.3   DEFINITIONS

         Quality Manual—Definitions of Terms

1.4   REFERENCES

Quality Manual

International Organization for Standardization ISO 9001–1994, Quality systems—Model for quality assurance in design/development, production, installation, and servicing.

International Organization for Standardization ISO 9000.3–1991, Guidelines for the application of ISO 9001 to the development, supply, and maintenance of software.

1.5   RESPONSIBILITIES

1.5.1   Preparation and Revision

The preparation and revision of quality management system procedures shall be performed by individuals nominated by the management representative. The work shall be managed by the management representative who is the custodian of all quality management system procedures.

1.5.2   Approval and Implementation

Quality management system procedures shall be approved and implemented by the management representative.

1.5.3   Distribution

Quality management system procedures shall be issued under the instruction of the chief executive officer or delegate and distributed in conformance with Product Management.

Procedures issued for information to persons other than registered holders of a Quality Procedures Manual shall be clearly marked:

UNCONTROLLED COPY—NOT SUBJECT TO CHANGE CONTROL

Each registered holder of a Quality Procedures Manual shall maintain his or her copy up to date in accordance with the Issue Status and Table of Contents.

1.6   PROCEDURE

1.6.1   General

Quality procedures describe the individual components of the quality management system and are intended to implement the policies stated in the Quality Manual and satisfy the requirements of ISO 9001. The procedures do not necessarily provide all the detailed instructions required to accomplish a specific quality-related task. Such detailed instructions or specifications are available from the Development Methodology, issued as required for each project as part of the Project Quality Plan or as project-specific standards and procedures.

1.6.2 Format

All quality procedures shall follow the format of this procedure. For identification of amendments each page contains an issue number, procedure identifier, and a page number within the procedure. Changes will be issued only as complete replacement procedures in accordance with Configuration Management procedures.

Procedures relating to compliance with ISO 9001 shall have the letters QP followed by a four-digit number. Other procedures shall have three alphabetic characters followed by three numeric characters. The management representative shall allocate procedure identifiers.

1.6.3 Change Control

All changes to Quality Procedures shall be issued as new procedures under the instruction of the management representative and distributed in conformance with Configuration Management procedures.

1.6.4 Section Contents

Each procedure shall contain the following sections:

- PURPOSE
  This section shall clearly and concisely explain the specific aim(s) of the procedure.

- SCOPE
  This section defines the coverage of the procedure in terms of what is covered (and is not covered) by the procedure.

- DEFINITIONS
  Words and terms used in the procedure that may cause confusion shall be defined or reference made to relevant documents.

- REFERENCES
  Bibliography of Standards and other documents referenced in the procedure.
- RESPONSIBILITIES
  Defines who is responsible for what. This specifically includes who does the work (follows the procedure), who reviews the work (if required), and who approves the work as being completed.
- PROCEDURE
  Describes how the work (executing the procedure) is to be done.
- RECORDS
  Describes which records or forms are used and retained to prove that the procedure has been followed.

1.6.5 Preparation

Quality Procedures will be prepared in the following manner:

- DRAFT PROCEDURE
  Following preparation by the nominated individual, the management representative shall provide a copy of each new or revised procedure to the relevant manager(s). Further copies for review shall be arranged by the manager(s).
- REVIEW PROCEDURE
  Persons to whom a draft is issued shall review the draft within 10 working days and pass comments to their manager. The manager shall consolidate the comments and pass them to the management representative within 15 working days of receipt of the draft.
- FINAL PROCEDURE
  The management representative shall resolve all input comments and prepare the final procedure. The chief executive officer or delegate and the management representative shall approve the release of the procedure.
- DISTRIBUTION
  All registered holders of the Quality Procedures Manual shall be issued with a copy of the new

procedure in accordance with Configuration Management procedures. Procedures issued for information to persons other than registered holders of the Quality Procedures Manual shall be clearly marked:

UNCONTROLLED COPY—NOT SUBJECT TO CHANGE CONTROL

1.6.6 Maintenance

Each procedure is to be reviewed at least once each year to determine that it is still adequate and relevant. These reviews shall be part of the quality management system review described in the Quality Manual.

Any revisions to procedures shall be prepared in accordance with this procedure.

1.7 RECORDS

The output from this procedure is a new or changed procedure, which will form part of the quality management system and will be published in the Quality Procedures Manual.

SOFTWARE DEVELOPMENT METHODOLOGY

The software development methodology should have a structure of what has to be done and what must be controlled to develop a system. How it has to be done can be left to the tools and techniques. This separation of *what* from *how* allows continuous improvement of process (the how) to occur while retaining the stability and experience of the methodology (the what). In other words, think of the methodology as being the structure within which you deploy the technology you intend to use in each project.

TOOLS, TECHNIQUES, AND STANDARDS

Tools, techniques, and standards include case tools, project-specific standards, analysis, programming and design techniques; these should be undergoing change, development, and improvement. When you use externally purchased products you should be looking at upgrading or replacement with something better. However, if you go for new tools, remember to prove that they work and yield cost-effective improvement before fully committing to them.

30

Developing the QMS

INTRODUCTION

If you are required to demonstrate the improvement gained by the implementation of a quality management system, you must not start the development process until you have gathered the baseline data. The reason is that the process of developing a quality management system starts to impact the existing process and pay dividends long before the formal system is accepted and implemented.

Make sure you continue through to certification to ensure that what you put in place is permanent and ongoing (certification helps achieve this) rather than a short-term payoff before slipping back (by inaction and lack of change) into the bad old ways. Trying to repeat the process after not following through the first time will be an incredibly difficult undertaking.

Developing your quality management systems is essentially a matter of documenting your existing processes and having the documentation agreed on and accepted by your people. Once they accept the documented process you need to gain acceptance for generating evidence that the process is being followed if your current process does not already generate evidence. You should at all times be looking to get your people involved in this process by asking them to fix, or correct, or change the documented processes. This leads them to assume ownership of the processes and therefore increases their acceptance of them. You will then need to examine your processes and identify gaps between your processes and the requirements of ISO 9001. Seek the help of your people in filling the gaps with suitable processes and ensure these are documented and that they generate suitable evidence. Once this is in place look at documenting the policies behind the processes if this has not already been done and produce the quality manual. Verify the implementation and the suitability of the processes with internal audits and management review. If it all looks satisfactory, seek certification. Once you have achieved certification you will find the system starts to look after itself with management review, corrective action, and internal quality system audits constantly refining and improving the processes. The following sections discuss the development and implementation process as a structured project.

PLANNING

The planning phase is designed to initiate the quality management system project and prepare and agree on the quality management system implementation plan. The project should start with an initial management team meeting. Prepare an agenda arranging the meeting and include material to make sure that the management team meetings become the process of management review as called for in ISO 9001. The initial management team meeting introduces the management team to quality management systems and the standards (ISO 9001, ISO 9000.3, and IEEE 1298). The next step is to provide a practical example of the development of the quality management system by formulating the management review policy and process and then using these to initiate the project. Finally, the management team needs to broadly agree on the contents of the quality management system implementation plan and agree on a series of management interviews and, where possible, schedule these interviews. The minutes of this meeting become the first record of the new quality management system.

Management interviews are then conducted to determine the organization structure, the products and services, the customers (internal and external), the capabilities to be covered by the certification, the processes to deliver the products or services, the technology in use, any existing documented processes, any current problem areas, and areas for improvement.

The broad findings are used to develop a plan for the design, development, and implementation of the quality management system, which takes into account existing processes and documentation and includes costs and schedule for the implementation. If the schedule is over twelve months the scope and coverage should be reviewed with a target of achieving certification for some capabilities within six to nine months. Other capabilities can then be introduced in subsequent assessments. The reason for keeping the project to less than twelve months is to maintain the focus and impetus necessary to achieve a result. Projects that go over twelve months often lose momentum and go stale. The quality management system implementation plan should then be processed through the sort of review and acceptance that will become the norm once the quality management system is implemented. This starts to get the management team into the structured formality that is required and enables them to set the tone for the level of bureaucracy they will later impose on the rest of the organization. When the plan has been accepted by the management team it should then be released as the baseline for developing your quality management system.

DEVELOPMENT

During development we acquire and create the physical documentation of the quality management system. During development we should also be implementing the processes as they are documented. If this is not feasible it suggests that the processes being documented are different from the way you work now and that there is, therefore, a possibility that you are throwing away the way you presently work and are replacing it with the way you think things should be done. This is a potentially dangerous way to proceed. It is far better to document your existing processes and then change them under controlled (corrective-action) processes than to assume you are doing things wrong now. If you are in business, have reasonably satisfied customers and are moving into formalized management systems, you are probably doing reasonably well already. Some processes will be new and will need formal implementation, but these will probably be left until you have documented your existing processes.

This phase generates the quality manual and the documented procedures, methods, work instructions, processes, standards, and guidelines. As each process is documented it should be reviewed by the affected staff, who should be encouraged to revise and change the documentation. This is a way by which the affected staff develop a feeling of ownership of the processes. In fact, you should go out of your way to include requested changes even if you feel they are wrong. There are three possibilities: The first is that you are wrong and therefore you should be grateful for the change; the second is that the affected staff are wrong but in this case they are at least establishing ownership and the process can be refined later; the third possibility is that both of you are wrong and ownership and correction will occur anyway. All in all, the benefits to be gained from the acceptance of processes by your people more than outweigh the occasional times that you are right and they are wrong.

Prior to commencing the documentation of the quality management system you should be sure all your people are briefed in what is going on and what the system is going to achieve. You will be seen to be implementing major change and there will be significant trepidation among your people. This is a natural reaction; they must be sold on the idea that you are looking to help and support them in working together to improve their jobs, their future, and their participation in the organization. One of the hardest sales points is that of encouraging the identification of problems and defects. Unless you are already well known to your people as a supporter of change and analysis of problems, there will be concern that you are trying to find out who causes the most problems with the intent of getting rid of them.

The starting point is to draft the quality policy statement and progress it through to signature by the relevant executive. This will be a fairly long process as many managers are more used to having other people bound by the written word than being bound to it themselves. Next, draft the organizational roles, responsibilities, and relationships and start progressing it to acceptance by the relevant managers.

Examine existing processes and, including the information provided by the management interviews, prepare a first-draft structure and outline of a quality manual. Obtain copies of all processes, procedures, methods, guidelines, and standards used within the organization and make sure policies are documented to prescribe their use. Review the content of the draft-quality manual with the management review team and revise the draft until it is accepted. The first version of the quality manual can then be issued as a baseline for development of the processes. This manual should not be considered engraved in stone; rather it should be seen as the starting point for processes and open to change.

Writing a quality manual is not an end in itself. It is a working document that defines and describes a system of management that is understood, agreed to, and complied with by all staff. It is imperative that you describe your own quality management system in your quality manual.

A good quality manual will provide documented evidence of a management system dedicated to consistently achieving specified quality objectives. It will facilitate understanding of the quality management system and engender commitment to it by all levels of management and staff. It will enable prospects, customers, end users, and third parties to perform assessments, audits, and evaluations to assure that your quality management system meets the requirements of the standards. And it will provide a reference source and be a training aid on policy for all management and staff.

The processes should then be documented using as much of the existing material as possible and changing this only when agreed to by the people who follow the process. For undocumented processes you should draft information based on interview and observation, but leave plenty of room for your people to correct and refine the process. This will help them to identify with the process and assume ownership of it. Make sure processes are documented as required to implement the policies in the quality manual. Make sure there are roadmaps to indicate what process is to be used when and where. In some cases this may be as simple as having the process physically located at the workstation where the process is to be performed. In the case of project work there will need to be a plan that will specify which processes are to be followed when, and by whom, to achieve the objectives of the project. Other processes will be triggered by events such as change requests, problem reports, need to purchase goods or services, or a new person starting work.

As procedures are being finalized, confirm that there will be suitable evidence in the form of records or other data that the procedure has been properly performed; also develop a checklist to be used during internal quality system audits.

While this documentation process is occurring do not prevent your people from adopting any new or revised procedures. You do not have to wait for some magical implementation date to start doing the right thing; if you are documenting properly, people should be keen to try the new approaches or formalize the existing ones.

Issue the draft process documentation to peer reviewers, supervisors, and management for final changes before acceptance and issue. Update the quality manual to reflect changes agreed to during process documentation. Finalize authorization of the documentation and prepare for formal implementation.

IMPLEMENTATION

Implementing a quality management system is both difficult and straightforward. It is difficult because everyone expects huge amounts of training and special coaching and will not accept anything less. It is straightforward because we should really only be confirming with our people that the way they have been doing things is basically the way they should now be doing them. The major issue in implementation is getting people used to having the process documented and requiring them to follow the documented process until it is changed, usually at their request but sometimes because of customer or design changes. In other words, we need to teach people how to deal with constant change, but implemented in a controlled and documented manner rather than for no apparent reason.

One of the most difficult jobs in implementation is convincing people that it is not difficult. If your system is basically a documentation of what you do now and has been documented in conjunction with the people who follow the processes, they are probably already following the documented processes. If you need training sessions to tell people how to do the job they are doing now, there is something seriously wrong with your organization. If your process documentation needs special training sessions so that people can understand it, it was obviously not documented for its intended users. We should be redocumenting the process, not teaching people to follow something where they need to remember the training rather than understand the process.

If you intend to have formalized, structured implementation, you will need to develop training material based on the process documentation. This should be used to draw out involvement of the trainees rather than for training them in the specifics of the process. When you are ready for implementation you should examine the organization and workload before scheduling the training sessions. You can then conduct the training sessions taking stock of how well the informal implementation (people using the processes after they have approved them) has progressed. The training sessions should draw on people's own experiences and call on them to identify where they fit into a process. This should be done as an open-book session; you are seeking their commitment and participation, not examining their memories. Encourage them to read the relevant part of the documentation or hold up the relevant visual aid to show what they are doing within the process. Encourage the team to support the person trying to explain the process. Get them all participating in the reading and explanation. Do not forget to have your own notetaker there to record the criticisms and improvements that will certainly come from well-run, enjoyable sessions.

CERTIFICATION

The validation of the success of the implementation phase of the quality management system comes from the certification of your quality management system. This is not some long-term, hard-to-achieve goal, but an independent examination of your quality management system to verify that it meets the requirements of ISO 9001 and is generally being followed by your people. When you have passed your ISO 9001 certification you know you are on the right track and can stop worrying about ISO 9001 and start concentrating on improving your system and processes. The ISO 9001 certification should be scheduled for about three months after the implementation sessions. This provides enough time for sufficient evidence of compliance to be generated and not enough time for your system to become rigid. Delaying certification for too long means that you will be resistant to changing your system lest you change it the wrong way. Instead of flexibility, you end up with the sort of bureaucratic rigidity that is the antithesis of constantly improving quality management systems. Remember to conduct internal quality systems audits as well as an occasional check of your system against the requirements of ISO 9001. Your selected certification agency or your consultant could be used to provide the check against ISO 9001 in order for you to concentrate on whether your people are conforming to your system rather than conforming to ISO 9001. You will also need to ensure continuing management commitment as evidenced by productive, participative management review meetings.

Prior to certification you should select a suitable certification agency based on your needs and your customers' expectations (see Chapter 31). Note that the credibility of your certification agency is of the utmost importance to the credibility of your certificate. Once you have selected your certification agency you will need to provide them with copies of your quality management system documentation. This will be reviewed for conformance with ISO 9001 and written feedback provided. The certification agency will then conduct a preliminary visit where they will discuss your documentation and observe your system in operation. If they are satisfied that you appear to be conforming to your system and that the documentation appears to satisfy ISO 9001 they will confirm the scheduled dates for the initial assessment.

The initial assessment will involve a team of assessors, possibly accompanied by technical experts, examining all parts of your quality management system for compliance with ISO 9001 and to make sure that your people are generally conforming to your system. While failure to address a requirement of ISO 9001 will prevent your achieving certification the problem may often be easily remedied and certification granted a few weeks later. If there are only minor failures to conform, certification may be granted immediately. You will usually be informed on the last day of the assessment if you are being recommended for certification. This may be contingent on responding to certain minor nonconformances to your documentation and minor misinterpretation of ISO 9001. Certification will need to be confirmed by the relevant management within the certification agency as well as by approval from the accreditation body under whose rules certification was conducted. (Chapter 31 explains this in more detail.)

POST IMPLEMENTATION

Following certification there is obviously the need to continue improving and developing your quality management system. In fact it is often only after certification that you feel confident enough to start changing the system and learning to make it fit your organization more comfortably. The transition from a formalized quality management system that everyone follows to a system that is perceived by all your people as "the way we do things around here" may take from two to five years and is the change to a *quality culture*. Waiting for this culture change before certification is a futile exercise because you will end up with a rigid system that you are scared to change in case it jeopardizes certification, instead of a relaxed, comfortable system where everybody knows they are part of a system that they control. The ongoing post implementation phase sees us continuing with management reviews, corrective action, and internal quality systems audits and using these to constantly improve our processes, products, and services.

31

Certification

CAPABILITY STATEMENTS

An organization is not certificated per se. Certification covers the capability of a group in one or more fields of endeavor. For example, certification may cover one organization, many organizations in one location, or a branch or a division of an organization. The capability may range from design and development of software to a full-service computing organization, including design, development, installation, support, and operation.

The capability statement for an organization tells you what they can (and cannot) do within the claim of certification.

Products cannot be certificated to ISO 9001 and there must be no suggestion in any advertisement that products are certificated. In fact, many certification agencies require all advertisements to be approved by them before use.

ACCREDITATION

Accreditation bodies may be established at government level within countries that subscribe to the ISO 9000 series of standards. These bodies accredit agencies to certificate organizations to the ISO 9000 series of standards. The certification process and the qualifications of assessors is defined in various documents and standards, including ISO 10011. Well-known accreditation bodies are:

- NACCB (National Accreditation Council for Certification Bodies)—UK.
- RAB (Registrar Accreditation Board)—US (for US-owned organizations only)
- RvC (Raad voor de Certificatie)—Netherlands.
- JAS–ANZ (Joint Accreditation System—Australia and New Zealand).

The role of the accreditation bodies is to maintain the standards of independence, certification, and auditing required by certification agencies. They evaluate and accredit certification agencies as achieving a level of competence to certificate the capabilities of organizations. The capabilities the certification agency can certificate are defined in their scope of accreditation. We are therefore looking at certification agencies whose scope of accreditation includes software development.

It is important to be aware that, although there are international standards, there is as yet no international body validating the credentials of accreditation bodies or certification agencies.

CERTIFICATION

When you have documented your quality management system and want independent verification and recognition that the system meets the requirement of ISO 9001, you should engage the services of a certification agency. The role of the certification agency is to assess the management system operating in the areas of nominated capabilities for compliance to the selected standard. If the system is found to be conforming, then the certification agency will issue a certificate of conformance. This certificate is valid for three years and requires six monthly surveillance audits during this period.

The selection of an agency and their scheduling of assessments takes about three months. This should be sufficient time for you to have exercised each process and have produced at least one copy of each form, record, or document your system calls for. Remember that each process implemented to meet the requirements of ISO 9001 must produce some evidence that it has been followed. Processes outside of the ISO 9001 requirements for the capability you want certificated will not be examined by your assessor.

Your certification agency will request copies of your quality management system documentation, which will be examined for conformance to ISO 9001. The agency will then visit you and discuss their findings on your documentation. During this visit they will examine some records and processes and then advise you if, in their opinion, you are ready for the certification audit.

Agencies that offer certification include:

- National standards bodies such as British Standards Institute, Standards Australia, Standards Association of New Zealand, Standards and Industrial Research Institute of Malaysia, and Singapore Institute of Standards and Industrial Research.
- Underwriters Laboratories (US).
- Det Norske Veritas (International).
- Bureau Veritas (International).
- Lloyds Register (International).
- SGS (International).

Nationally based certification agencies are entering into a variety of agreements to provide a form of international coverage. Two such types of arrangements are:

- Memoranda of understanding to recognize each other's certifications and allow, for example, an Australian-certificated company to be listed on the British Standards register.
- Contracts whereby assessments done by one agency's assessors are accepted as if they were done by the other agency; for example, between Australia and New Zealand standards associations.

When an organization is certificated by an accredited certification agency the logo of the accreditation body will be included in the certificate as evidence that the certification was performed in accordance with the standards and procedures laid down by that accreditation body.

REGISTRATION

The details of the certificated organization, the standard to which it is certificated, and the capabilities certificated are listed in one or more registers of certificated organizations. Each certification agency operates its own register. Additionally, the UK DTI (Department of Trade and Industry) operates a register of all organizations certificated by agencies accredited by the NACCB. The registration of certificated organizations is an area of concern in that there are few, if any, national registers. For instance, if a foreigner wishes to do business in Singapore, Australia, or New Zealand there is no single source of information on all certificated organizations in those countries. It is necessary to contact each certification agency (if you know them all) and ask for information on organizations they have certificated.

Because the number of certificated organizations is growing at a very high rate the registers may be significantly out of date and a direct approach may be required to a likely organization to obtain a copy of its certificate.

In conjunction with the internationalization of the ISO 9000 standards there are a number of coregistration agreements in force between national registers. This allows organizations listed on one of these registers to have their registration (and capability) listed on other participants' registers. The registration fee is usually about $1,000 per application and $1,000 per annum. The coregistration agreements include:

- Standards Australia
- Standards Association of New Zealand
- British Standards Institute
- Standards Institute of Israel
- Swiss Association for Quality Assurance Certificates
- Japan Machinery and Metals Inspection Institute
- Underwriters Laboratories (US)
- Quality Management Institute (Canada)

SELECTING A CERTIFICATION AGENCY

Selecting a certification agency should take into account where and with whom you want to do business; the geographical spread of your business; your personal relationship with the lead assessor; and the politics internal and external to your organization.

Essentially, the selection of a certification agency is a normal business decision that should be based strongly on value for money rather than low price.

The major issue to be addressed is the perception of your customer. Would your customer have faith in the credentials of your certification agency and their accreditation body? For example, would an American buyer have confidence in a certificate issued by a Panama-based certification agency? To this end, the certification agencies put a lot of effort into establishing and maintaining their bonafide and credibility. Many certification agencies are building on reputations of hundreds of years of service to their customers.

Here is the way to select your agency:

- Examine your market and its perception of the credibility of the various agencies you may use.
- Prepare a short list of suitable agencies.
- Contact the local office of the agency and obtain literature on their services.
- Complete the questionnaire that is provided—this questionnaire is required for them to prepare a quotation for the services you need.
- Arrange a meeting with the agency. At this meeting you should ask to meet the lead assessor who will look after your organization. Discuss the services offered, particularly as they apply to you. The completed questionnaire will give you a basis for the meeting.
- Decide which agencies you would be comfortable working with and submit the questionnaire for preparation of a quotation.
- Evaluate the quotations based on the overall three-year cost of obtaining and maintaining the certificate and select an agency.
- Courtesy suggests you inform unsuccessful agencies of the reason you did not select them—this will enable them to improve the quality and value of their services to future clients.

Quality Terminology

Accepted The recorded decision that a product has satisfied the requirements and may be delivered to the customer or used in the next part of the process.

Approved The recorded decision that the product or part of the product has satisfied your quality standards.

Authorized The recorded decision that the product or record has been cleared for use or action.

Contract The order, contract, agreement, or understanding between a customer and a developer to develop or maintain a product. This may not be a formal written document, although the quality plan that embodies the contract should be accepted by both parties.

Customer The person or organization for whom we are producing the product. The customer may be an in-house user or an external organization.

Documentation Product Any report, manual, specification, or other documented work developed as part of a contract or supplied by a customer for use on a contract.

Grade An indicator of category or rank related to features or characteristics that cover different sets of needs for products or services intended for the same functional use. Grade reflects a planned or recognized difference in requirements.

Inspection Verification.

Purchaser Customer.

Quality   The totality of features and characteristics of a product or service that bear on its ability to satisfy stated or implied needs. Customer's needs are usually translated into features and characteristics with specified criteria. Needs may include aspects of usability, safety, availability, reliability, maintainability, economics, and environment. Needs must be specified in such a manner that we know when we have satisfied them (they must be testable). The term *quality* is not an expression of a degree of excellence.

Quality Assurance   All those planned and systematic actions necessary to provide adequate confidence that a product or service will satisfy given requirements for quality.

Quality Audit   A systematic independent examination to determine whether quality activities and related results comply with planned arrangements and whether these arrangements are implemented effectively and are suitable to achieve objectives.

Quality Control   The operational techniques and activities that are used to fulfill requirements for quality. Quality control involves operational techniques and activities aimed both at monitoring a process and at eliminating causes of unsatisfactory performance.

Quality Management   Includes strategic planning, allocation of resources, and other systematic activities for quality, such as quality planning, operations, and evaluations.

Quality Policy   That aspect of the overall management function that determines and implements the quality policy. While achieving desired quality requires the commitment and participation of everybody in the organization the responsibility for quality management belongs to top management.

Quality System   The organizational structure, responsibilities, procedures, processes, and resources for implementing quality management. The quality system should be only as comprehensive as needed to meet quality objectives.

Quality System Review   A formal evaluation by top management of the status and adequacy of the quality system in relation to quality policy and the definition of new objectives to be achieved as a result of business changes.

Subcontractor   A party whom we have contracted to produce product on behalf of our customer. The subcontractor is then our supplier and we are the subcontractor's customer.

Supplier   The person or organization producing the product.

Testing   Validation.

Test Specification   Describes the test criteria and the methods to be used in a specific test to assure the performance and design specifications have been satisfied. The test specification identifies the capabilities or program functions to be tested and identifies the test environment.

Validation   The process of evaluating a product or service to ensure compliance with the specified requirements.

Verification   The process of evaluating a product or service at a point in the process (or at the end of the process) to ensure correctness and consistency with respect to the products and standards provided as input to that process.

Checklist

The following checklist summarizes the issues and should be used during the development of your quality management system (QMS) to gauge your compliance to ISO 9001. Your assessor may use a different checklist, so there is no guarantee of total compliance. You should be able to point to your quality management system documentation to show where the question is answered and, where applicable, point to a record that demonstrates that the specified process was followed.

MANAGEMENT RESPONSIBILITY

- What is the status of the quality manual?
- Is there a quality policy?
- Who authorized the quality policy?
- How is the quality policy distributed to all levels of the organization?
- Does the manual contain reference to procedures for the elements in the ISO 9001:
  - Organization?
  - Management Review?
  - Documentation?
  - Contract Review?
  - Design Control?
  - Document Control?
  - Purchasing Control?
  - Customer-Supplied Product?

- • Traceability and Configuration Management?
- • Process Control?
- • Inspection and Testing?
- • Inspection and Test Equipment?
- • Inspection and Test Status?
- • Nonconforming Product Control?
- • Corrective Action?
- • Handling Storage Packaging, Preservation, and Delivery?
- • Installation/Implementation?
- • Quality Records?
- • Internal Quality Audits?
- • Training?
- • Servicing/Maintenance?
- • Statistical Techniques?
- Is an organization chart available?
- Are roles and responsibilities recorded for functions/areas doing work affecting quality?
- Are relationships between functions/areas clearly defined and documented?
- Are job descriptions available for major roles in areas affecting quality?
- Is there a formalized system to ensure that trained personnel equipped with suitable resources are identified for performing work, verification of work, and management of work?
- Is a management representative appointed having defined authority and responsibility for ensuring the requirements of the QMS are met?
- Is the management representative a member of the executive?
- Are records of management reviews of the quality system available?
- Is there a means to define the customer's responsibilities?
- Does the system provide for joint reviews to be scheduled for:
  - • Ensuring developed software meets the requirements specification?
  - • Reviewing verification results?
  - • Acceptance of test results?

QUALITY SYSTEM

- Are there documented procedures?
- Are there documented methods?
- Are there documented standards?

- Is the basis of the QMS defined?
- Are definitions recorded?
- Is there a list of procedures?
- Is a quality plan generated for each project?

PROPOSALS AND CONTRACT REVIEW

- Does a formal system exist for proposal preparation?
- Does the system provide for proposals to be reviewed by qualified personnel?
- Does the system provide for proposals to be authorized before issue?
- Does a formal system exist for review of contracts?
- Does the system ensure records are kept of contract reviews?
- Does the system allow for review of the contract by qualified persons?
- Does the system ensure:
    - The requirements are adequately defined and documented?
    - That differences between tender and contract documents are identified?
    - The capability to meet the contract is confirmed?
- Does the system ensure terminology is agreed on by both parties?
- Does the system allow for review of customers' capability to meet their side of the contract?

DESIGN CONTROL

- Does a formal method exist for preparing requirements specifications?
- Does the specification method provide a means for consultation with the customer to resolve ambiguities, errors, and omissions?
- Does the specification method provide a means to ensure that the specification defines the requirements?
- Does the specification method provide a means to ensure that the customer accepts the specification?
- Does the specification method provide a means to analyze the requirements to ensure they are feasible and testable?
- Does a formal system exist to plan the design/development activity?
- Does the system assign responsibility for activities?
- Does the system require a review to be performed of the resources required?
- Does the system allow for identification of organization and technical interfaces and exchange of information?
- Does the system permit changes as the design/development evolves?

- Does the system provide for design input requirements relating to the product/service to be recorded and reviewed in a formalized manner?
- Does the system allow for clarification of incomplete, ambiguous, or conflicting requirements with the person who originally specified the requirements?
- Does the system require the final design to be documented?
- Does the system require the final design to be expressed such that deliverables can be related to the requirements specification?
- Does the system require that the design output contain or reference acceptance criteria?
- Does the system require a review of relevant statutory requirements?
- Does the system require the design to identify those characteristics that are crucial to safe and proper functioning of the product/service?
- Is there a formal process for performing design reviews?
- Does the system require design reviews be documented?
- Is there a mechanism to identify persons who can participate in design reviews?
- Does the system require the design reviewer(s) have sufficient independence/detachment from the design originator?
- Does the design review procedure include:
  - The objectives of each review?
  - Identification of review points?
  - Methods for specifying nonscheduled reviews?
  - Identification of the job functions of the reviewer(s)?
  - Provision for recording and analysis of recommendations of reviews?
  - Means to ensure recommendations are processed in a timely manner?
- Are design verification measures provided to ensure the deliverable meets the requirements specification, such as:
  - Tests and demonstrations?
  - Use of alternative calculations or empirical formula?
  - Comparison with similar or proven designs?
  - Feedback from installation, commissioning, and servicing functions?
- Are formal procedures laid down for the review, approval, and issue of design changes?
- Are programming standards documented?
- Are documentation product standards documented?
- Are there procedures to review programming and documentation product for compliance with standards and with design criteria?

- Is there a formal system for reviewing programming to ensure it is comprehensible, testable, and maintainable?
- Do programming standards describe approved programming practices and list any prohibited practices relevant to the language being used?
- Do programming standards cover all areas such as program design, coding, program testing and inspection, integration, and program documentation?

QMS DOCUMENTATION CONTROL

- Is there a system to control the issue and updating of documentation relevant to the standards (QMS documentation)?
- Does the system ensure approval before issue of the above?
- Does the system ensure effective distribution of documents?
- Does the system ensure obsolete documents are removed from all points of issue or use?
- Does the system ensure changes to documents are approved by the originating function?
- If changes are not approved by the origination function, does the system require that the designated change control function have access to pertinent background information?
- Does the system allow for the recording of changes to documentation?
- Does the system require a master list or similar mechanism to identify the status of documents?

PURCHASING

- Does the system require a formal list of approved suppliers/contractors?
- Is there a formal procedure for the assessment and monitoring of suppliers/contractors?
- Are suitable functions required to be involved in the assessment review of subcontractors?
- Does the system require internal quality audits to include subcontractors' quality assurance systems?
- Does the system require records be maintained of monitoring/assessments of subcontractors?
- Does the system ensure that the purchasing documentation contains complete and precise information?
- Does the system require purchasing documents to be checked and reviewed prior to release?

- Does the system have procedures to identify the implication of customer verification requirements?

CUSTOMER-SUPPLIED PRODUCT

- Is there a system for the verification of customer-supplied products?
- Is there a system to report the loss, damage, or unsuitability of customer-supplier products?
- Is there a system to safeguard and maintain customer-supplied product?
- Does the system require a register of customer-supplied products?

PRODUCT IDENTIFICATION AND TRACEABILITY

- Are there procedures for identifying the product from specifications during development, delivery, and installation?
- Is there a system to uniquely identify and record product for traceability?
- Is there a system to identify and control software components and deliverable documentation including changes?
- Do configuration management procedures include:
  - Version identification, issue, and control?
  - Obtaining approval to implement modifications?
  - Ensuring modifications are properly integrated through formal change control?

PLANNING AND PROCESS CONTROL

- Does a formal system exist for planning projects?
- Do the plans include:
  - Organizational and technical interfaces?
  - Quality issues, including:
    - Standards, procedures, and methods?
    - Inspection and testing tools?
    - Development cycle?
    - Review, inspection, and test requirements?
    - Development environment?
  - Development plan, including:
    - Phases?
    - Management?
    - Methods and tools?
    - Process control?

- Phase input?
- Phase output?
- Verification of phases?
- Test plan?
- Installation and implementation plan?
- Product management plan?
- Postinstallation maintenance plan?
- Project plan (resources, schedules, and costs)?
- Does the system require plans be reviewed by qualified personnel?
- Does the system require plans be authorized before issue?
- Is there a system to plan production, and where applicable, installation?
- Is there a requirement for the planning to define the requirements for design/development and production/installation equipment?
- Does the system require reference to standards, quality plan, and workmanship criteria?
- Does the system require the work be carried out in a suitable, and where applicable, controlled environment?
- Does the system ensure that manufacture takes place with equipment and processes approved and suitable for that product/process?
- Are work instructions and procedures prepared to define the manner of production and installation?
- Do the work instructions make reference to standards codes, quality plan, and workmanship criteria where applicable?
- Does the system require work instructions and procedures to be systematically reviewed?
- Does the system require processes and product characteristics to be monitored during production/installation?
- Are systems in existence for monitoring and controlling special processes, such as software development?
- Does the system require personnel performing work on special processes to be adequately trained and qualified?
- Does the system require records be maintained for qualified processes, equipment, and personnel?

INSPECTION AND TEST

- Do procedures state the nature and extent of inspection (e.g., from requirements through design/development, production, and installation)?
- Does the system require verification that the product/service conforms to specified requirements?

- Does the system hold the product until conformance is verified except under positive recall?
- Do procedures ensure identification of nonconforming products/ services?
- Does a documented system exist for inspection at the goods-receiving centers?
- Does the system require adequate information be provided for the inspection of the product/service and its related documentation?
- Does the system ensure that all previous inspection and tests have been carried out and that the results are acceptable?
- Does a procedure exist to carry out final inspection in accordance with requirements (e.g., quality plan, specification, drawing)?
- Does the system require all final inspection results be recorded and the records authorized?
- Does the system ensure that final inspection is performed before dispatch?
- Does the system ensure that records are maintained, stating inspection results against defined acceptance criteria?

INSPECTION MEASURING AND TEST EQUIPMENT

- Does a system exist to register, calibrate, and maintain test and measuring equipment? This could include computer programs used to test (directly or indirectly) other programs.
- Does the system extend to hired and customer-supplied equipment?
- Are there documented procedures for different types of measuring and test equipment, including jigs and fixtures, to define acceptable criteria, frequency of checks, and action to be taken when results are unsatisfactory?
- Does the system require calibration records be maintained for inspection?
- Does the system assess and document the validity of previous inspection and test results when measuring and test equipment is found to be out of calibration?
- Does the system require the degree of uncertainty to be assessed against the required measurement accuracy?
- Does the system ensure that measurement uncertainty is recorded?
- Does the system require the environmental conditions be assessed and/or controlled for calibration and inspection?
- Does the system ensure recall/calibration in good time at prescribed intervals, or prior to use, against equipment traceable to a nationally recognized standard?

- Does the system require the measuring/test equipment be identified with a suitable indicator or approved identification record to show calibration status?
- Does the system require equipment (including software and hardware) be safeguarded to prevent adjustments that could invalidate the setting?
- Does the system require measuring and test equipment be stored and maintained under conditions ensuring accuracy and fitness for use?

INSPECTION AND TEST STATUS

- Does the system identify the inspection and test status of the product/service by a suitable means?
- Does the system require inspection and test records to identify who released the product/service as passing inspection or test?

NONCONFORMING PRODUCT

- Is there a system established and documented to ensure control of nonconforming products and documents?
- Does the system require nonconforming products be identified, marked, and if necessary, segregated to prevent inadvertent use or installation?
- Does the system define who has the responsibility and authority to decide the disposition of nonconformance and of external inspection and testing after repair, rework, or correction?
- Does the system have a mechanism for dealing with customer-granted concessions?
- Does the system require actions arising from the treatment of nonconformances be recorded?
- Does the system ensure that corrected or repaired products/services are reinspected?

CORRECTIVE AND PREVENTIVE ACTION

- Are there procedures established to investigate the cause of nonconforming products/services?
- Do the procedures include analysis of processes, work operations, concessions, quality records, complaints, and service reports to detect and eliminate potential causes of nonconforming products/services?

- Does the system require records of customer complaints be maintained?
- Does the system require preventative actions be taken to deal with deteriorating trends or problems?
- Does the system require management reviews of corrective action be carried out to ensure they are effective?
- Does the review system lead to revisions in procedures resulting from corrective action?

HANDLING, STORAGE, PACKAGING, PRESERVATION, AND DELIVERY

- Are procedures/instructions available detailing methods for handling, storage, packaging, and delivery of the products?
- Does the system require actions be taken to ensure that the identity/marking of material or product is retained in accordance with specified requirements until the supplier's responsibility ceases?
- Does the system cover product/material provided by the customer or subcontractor?
- Does the system require a secure storage area be provided with an environment to prevent any deterioration of the product?
- Do the procedures cover the authorized receipt and dispatch to and from such areas?
- Does the system require inspection of the condition of stored items be carried out on a formalized basis?
- Does the system require all shipments be prepared and transported in conformance to specified requirements?
- Does the system provide procedures for the delivery of services?
- Does the system provide procedures for installation and other contractual conditions?

QUALITY RECORDS

- Is a system established for the identification, collection, indexing, filing, storage, maintenance, and disposition of quality records?
- Does the system require records be readily retrievable?
- Does the system require inspection results to show if specified requirements have been achieved or nature of nonconformance?
- Does the system extend to subcontractor records?
- Does the system require retention times for records be established and recorded?
- Does the system require records be stored in an environment that will minimize deterioration or damage and prevent loss?
- Does the system allow for customer evaluation of the records?

INTERNAL QUALITY AUDITS

- Does the system for internal quality audits operate against a planned schedule?
- Does the system require the scope of each audit be clearly defined?
- Does the internal system extend to on-site activities?
- Does the system require the audit results be documented?
- Does the system require necessary corrective actions be initiated, reviewed, and closed out positively within a reasonable time scale?
- Does the system require audits be carried out by qualified personnel having sufficient independence and authority?

TRAINING

- Is there a system for the identification of training needs of all personnel?
- Does the system require education/training be provided where required?
- Does the system require training records be maintained?
- Does the system require records to contain details of education, training, and skills to be maintained for all personnel performing activities affecting quality?

SERVICING AND MAINTENANCE

- Do procedures exist for servicing?
- Do procedures exist for verifying that servicing meets the specified requirements?
- Does a mechanism exist to feed information to the design and manufacturing departments?
- Does the system require standards applied during maintenance be consistent with the standards and procedures used during software development?

STATISTICAL TECHNIQUES

- Does the system specify that the use of statistical techniques be approved for evaluating process, product, or service capabilities?
- Does the system ensure that the data from such techniques is reviewed and action taken where required?

Bibliography

Ackoff, R. L., 1987. *The Art of Problem Solving: Accompanied by Ackoff's Fables.* New York: Wiley-Interscience.

Albrecht, A., 1979. Measuring application development productivity. *Proceedings of the SHARE/GUIDE Application Development Conference.*

Babich, W., 1986. *Software Configuration Management.* Reading, MA: Addison-Wesley.

Bersoff, E., Henderson, V., and Siegel, S., 1980. *Software Configuration Management: An Investment in Product Integrity.* Englewood Cliffs, NJ: Prentice-Hall.

Bryan, W., and Siegel, S., 1988. *Software Product Assurance.* New York: Elsevier.

Buckle, J., 1982. *Software Configuration Management.* New York: Macmillan.

Buckley, F., and Poston, R., 1984. Software quality assurance. *IEEE Transactions on Software Engineering SE-10.*

Crosby, P., 1984. *Quality Without Tears.* New York: McGraw-Hill.

Crosby, P., 1979. *Quality is Free.* New York: McGraw-Hill.

DeBono, E., 1970. *Lateral Thinking.* New York: Harper & Row.

Deming, W. E., 1991. *Out of the Crisis.* Cambridge, MA: MIT CAES.

Dunn R., and Ullman, R., 1982. *Quality Assurance for Computer Software.* New York: McGraw-Hill.

EXECOM, 1993. *The APT Methodology.* EXECOM Group.

Glass, R. L., 1979. *Software Reliability Guidebook.* Englewood Cliffs, NJ: Prentice-Hall.

IEEE, 1993. Software engineering standards. *IEEE, Spring 1993 Edition.*

International Organization for Standardization, 1991. *ISO 8258, Shewhart control charts.* ISO or local standards body.

International Organization for Standardization, 1994. *ISO 8402, Quality—Vocabulary.* ISO or local standards body.

International Organization for Standardization, 1991. *ISO 9000.3, Quality Management and Quality System Elements—Guidelines for development, supply and maintenance of software.* ISO or local standards body.

International Organization for Standardization, 1993. *ISO 9001, Quality Systems—Model for quality assurance in design, development, production, installation and servicing.* ISO or local standards body.

International Organization for Standardization, 1989. *ISO 9004.2, Quality Management and Quality System Elements—Guidelines for services.* ISO or local standards body.

International Organization for Standardization, 1993. *ISO 9004.4, Guidelines for quality improvement.* ISO or local standards body.

International Organization for Standardization, 1991. *ISO 9126, Information Technology—Software Product Evaluation—Quality characteristics and guidelines for their use.* ISO or local standards body.

International Organization for Standardization, 1988. *ISO 10011, Guidelines for auditing quality systems.* ISO or local standards body.

International Organization for Standardization, 1992. *ISO 10013, Guidelines for developing quality manuals.* ISO or local standards body.

Jones, C., 1994. *Assessment and Control of Software Risks.* Englewood Cliffs, NJ: Yourden Press.

McConnel, J., 1991. *Safer Than a Known Way.* Englewood Cliffs, NJ: Prentice-Hall.

Paulk et al., 1993. *Key Practices of the Capability Maturity Model.* Pittsburg, PA: Software Engineering Institute.

Perry, W. E., 1977. *Effective Methods of EDP Quality Assurance.* Q.E.D Information Sciences.

Peters, T., 1989. *Thriving on Chaos.* London: Pan.

Scherkenbach, W. W., 1986. *Quality and Productivity, Road Maps and Road Blocks.* Washington, DC: Mercury.

Smith, D., and Wood K., 1989. *Engineering Quality Software,* 2nd Ed. New York: Elsevier.

Standards Australia, 1991. *AS 3563, Software Quality Management System, Parts 1 & 2.* Standards Australia, Sydney.

Watts, R., 1987. *Measuring Software Quality.* Manchester, UK: National Computing Centre.

Index